Anger ...
How Do You
Handle It?

About Ellel Ministries

Our Vision

Ellel Ministries is a non-denominational Christian Mission Organization with a vision to resource and equip the Church by welcoming people, teaching them about the Kingdom of God and healing those in need (Luke 9:11).

Our Mission

Our mission is to fulfill the above vision throughout the world, as God opens the doors, in accordance with the Great Commission of Jesus and the calling of the Church to proclaim the Kingdom of God by preaching the good news, healing the broken-hearted and setting the captives free. We are, therefore, committed to evangelism, healing, deliverance, discipleship and training. The particular scriptures on which our mission is founded are Isaiah 61:1–7; Matthew 28:18–20; Luke 9:1–2; 9:11; Ephesians 4:12; 2 Timothy 2:2.

Our Basis of Faith

God is a Trinity. God the Father loves all people. God the Son, Jesus Christ, is Savior and Healer, Lord and King. God the Holy Spirit indwells Christians and imparts the dynamic power by which they are enabled to continue Christ's ministry. The Bible is the divinely inspired authority in matters of faith, doctrine and conduct, and is the basis for teaching.

For more information

Please visit our website at www.ellelministries.org for full up-to-date information about the world-wide work of Ellel Ministries.

ELLEL MINISTRIES
THE TRUTH AND FREEDOM SERIES

Anger ...
How Do You
Handle It?

Paul and Liz Griffin

Sovereign World

Sovereign World Ltd
PO Box 784
Ellel
Lancaster LA1 9DA
England

Unless otherwise stated, all Scripture quotations are taken from the New
International Version. Copyright © 1973, 1978, 1984 by International Bible
Society.

NKJV – New King James Version, copyright © 1983, 1992 by Thomas
Nelson, Inc.

ISBN: 978 1 85240 450 5

The publishers aim to produce books which will help to extend and build up
the Kingdom of God. We do not necessarily agree with every view expressed
by the authors, or with every interpretation of Scripture expressed. We expect
readers to make their own judgment in the light of their understanding of
God's Word and in an attitude of Christian love and fellowship.
All the examples used in this book are real, but names and incidental details
have been altered to preserve the privacy of the individuals involved.

Cover design by Andy Taylor, Ellel Ministries
Typeset by CRB Associates, Reepham, Norfolk
Printed in Malta

Contents

Foreword

Anger can be a major hidden issue in many people's lives. It is often the cause of things getting out of control, leading to events which cause pain and suffering to other people and ongoing problems for the individual concerned. It is not unusual to find people, who desire to live a godly Christian life, struggling to understand why things consistently go wrong. So often the root cause is unresolved anger arising from earlier events in life, which if not faced and resolved will continue to be a source of difficulty and potential crisis.

I am delighted, therefore, that Paul and Liz Griffin have turned their many years of ministry and teaching experience into a book which faces this vital issue head on, but in such a way that does not put the reader into condemnation. The book helps people to understand what is happening and then see a way forward towards healing and restoration. Gaining knowledge and understanding of a problem is the most important step that anyone can take towards resolving it.

I pray that many people will find this excellent little book a great encouragement, as they see that they don't have to live with the problem of anger for the rest of their days. It will be a blessing to many.

Peter Horrobin
International Director of Ellel Ministries

About the Authors

For twenty years Paul and Liz lived as expatriates in South Africa, Bahrain and Japan. While Paul pursued his career as a chemical engineer with an international oil company, Liz, who trained as a primary school teacher, was a full-time mother bringing up their two children as well as being involved in many Christian activities and a volunteer telephone counselling service. A growing desire to serve the Lord led Paul to resign his job and enrol for a three-year Bible College course back in England. They became involved with Ellel Ministries in 1991 as part of the ministry team. They joined the full-time team at Ellel Grange in 1995. Paul is a member of the leadership team, and both Paul and Liz teach and minister to those seeking healing in their lives.

Preface

For most of us, the simple answer to the question posed in the title of this book *Anger ... How Do You Handle It?* is *"badly."* Many of us may not recognize we have a problem at all. Some of us will deny that we have a problem with handling anger and will blame others for our own reactions to all of life's inevitable frustrations. We may even be totally unaware that the way we handle this most powerful of emotions affects others.

> "Anger ... How do you handle it?"

We may defend the way we express our anger by claiming that our behavior is just part of our personality. Many of us struggle through life, trying to keep this emotion under control. Our lives are punctuated with episodes where we lose control and vent our feelings in ungodly and sinful ways. These are often followed by guilt and repentance, but without lasting change in behavior.

As the team at Ellel Ministries ministered into the lives of people seeking help, it became apparent that the inability to handle anger in godly ways is a key issue for many Christians. It affects our relationship with God and with others. It affects the way we think about ourselves. It is often a root cause of physical sickness and depression.

We discovered that few people had ever heard a sermon or any teaching on the subject of anger. We found that Christians had conflicting ideas on their interpretation of what the Bible has to say on this subject. There was little understanding as to the difference between righteous and unrighteous anger or how anger could be expressed in godly ways. The role of the demonic was often either ignored completely or over-emphasized. It was very apparent that there was a need for biblical and practical teaching on the subject.

There was some nervousness as we prepared to pioneer our first anger course at Ellel Grange in 1997. We had advertised the course widely and had no idea who might turn up. "Who in their right mind," we asked ourselves, "would want to get fifty angry people together under one roof for a whole weekend? Did we need to hide everything that wasn't screwed down in case anyone threw a temper tantrum? Did we need to seat some of our male team members in the front row to act as bodyguards for the speakers?"

> "Who in their right mind?" we asked ourselves,
> "would want to get fifty angry people together under
> one roof for a whole weekend?"

The people who arrived were not all "Incredible Hulk" look-a-likes. (A fictional television character, who would suddenly and unexpectedly transform from normality to an angry and raging monster.) They were just normal-looking Christians. People who knew, or in most cases had been told, that they were struggling with various problems associated with anger. Most of them were not angry looking at all, but rather, we were surprised to find, people who were out of touch with all of their emotions.

We watched with amazement as God brought understanding and deep healing into their lives. Feedback and testimonies, such as the following, were encouraging to us and we hope encouraging to you:

> "I've been struggling with anger. My dad was a very angry man, an alcoholic, quite abusive and I always felt it was my fault. God dealt with the whole thing and I can move on. I believe I was totally healed last night."

> "I've learned to understand anger. I've been an angry person most of my life. It's God that changes us. I've learned about good anger on this course."

> "When we prayed last night about memories and feelings being brought together, God showed me something. He brought back a memory of my dad speaking over me, telling me off for showing emotion. The counselor prayed and broke the power of those words. I'm just realizing today how much that has set me free."

> "I never felt angry for years, just didn't think I had any anger. The Lord revealed I had frozen anger. In situations in the past where I should have been angry I'd always blame myself and bury it. I'd get so angry with myself. God was dealing with this last night. I've had to deal with self-hatred."

The teaching and keys we share on our anger courses, and which have brought deep healing into many people's lives, are the basis for this book. As you read, you might like to imagine yourself joining in and put them into practice. Our prayer is that God will give you understanding and hope, and that your answer to the question *"Anger ... How Do You Handle It?"* will be, *"Much better than I did in the past."*

Paul and Liz Griffin
Ellel Grange, March 2006

CHAPTER 1

Anger ... How Do We Handle It?

As the meeting progressed, Brian, the young man sitting next to me (Paul), was becoming more and more agitated. The teacher was speaking about how God wants to bring healing into our lives, but Brian didn't seem capable of sitting still and listening. At first he began to shuffle his feet. Then he kept shifting his body position as if he could not make himself comfortable. Then I noticed that he had begun to clench his fists – the muscles in his neck had tightened and now stood out. The color of his face had changed and had taken on a pinkish hue. I was just wondering if he was all right when he leaned over and hissed, "I feel like walking out to the front of this meeting and throttling that speaker."

"I feel like throttling that speaker."

I was somewhat taken aback. It was my first healing retreat as part of the ministry team and I could not recall that handling counselees intent on murder had been covered in any of the training sessions. I had been told to be ready for anything, but I was not expecting this. The thought flashed through my mind that I probably wouldn't be on the ministry team too long if I

allowed the person I was supposed to be helping to attack the
preacher!

I started to pray fervently, whilst at the same time preparing
myself to make a flying rugby tackle, should he get up out of
his seat and start towards the front. This was really unfamiliar
ground because, at all the Christian events I had ever been to, I
had always hoped people would respond to the preaching and
go to the front! I found myself whispering back to the young
man, "Hold on a minute – he hasn't finished speaking yet."
These were, apparently, amazing words of wisdom (or was it
prayer?). They did the trick and he was able to simmer in his
anger, without trying to express it, for the rest of the meeting!
Thankfully he was able to get help for his problems through
the course of the healing retreat.

Joe's story

Joe was another young man I was trying to help who got in
touch with his anger during a teaching session on a healing
retreat. He couldn't cope with the teacher saying that we have
a heavenly Father who loves us. His experience of a father was
anything but someone who showed love. He knew all about
angry fathers. He knew about fathers who would beat you
black and blue for no reason. He knew about fathers that
you had to hide from when they came home drunk from the
pub. He knew about fathers who never had a good word to
say about you. He knew almost nothing about and had no
experience of a father who might care for you and want the
best for you.

> He knew all about angry fathers.

Suddenly he jumped out of his seat and stormed out into the
entrance hall of Ellel Grange with me following behind in close

pursuit. With a display of superhuman, or was it supernatural strength, he picked up the leather-covered Chesterfield arm-chair (which must have weighed nearly 200 pounds), raised it to head height, and tossed it across the hall. With this sudden release of anger he collapsed to the floor and began crying and sobbing uncontrollably as the memories of all the rejection he had received from his father came flooding to the surface. In an instant an angry, strong and violent young man had got in touch with the inner pain of a vulnerable hurting little boy. Later on, as we prayed together, he was able to experience the reality of God's love for him as a heavenly Father.

> He collapsed to the floor and began crying and sobbing uncontrollably.

Joyce's story

People handle their anger in different ways. Take Joyce, for instance. Joyce had run away from home in her early teens to escape the unwanted sexual advances from her mum's latest boyfriend. She had spent most of her short life living in foster homes, hostels or sleeping rough out on the streets. She had learnt to be independent and self-reliant and was obviously very rebellious.

> Inside she was seething with unrecognized anger.

Inside she was seething with unrecognized anger. She'd been to a few churches but they didn't know how to handle her. Her uncontrolled outbursts had led to her being banned from attending house-group meetings. The church was not too pleased, she told us with a smile, when on another occasion she had vented her rage on the beautiful floral display at the front of the church. Joyce showed little sign of repentance for her angry actions and felt they were a justifiable way of expressing her emotions.

Liz's story

It had been an eventful week. I (Liz) had gone to my weekly women's group feeling depressed and low. My friends prayed that God would fill me with His Holy Spirit. I was over-whelmed by the presence of God and spoke in tongues for the first time. Now, each day, instead of depression, I was filled with the joy of God. My friend Angela had also been touched by God and had decided to undergo full immersion baptism so I was excited for her as well.

> His face turned quite red and he became very angry.

I was still on a high when I bumped into the vicar. "Isn't it exciting," I enthused, "that Angela is going to get baptized next week?" I wasn't prepared for his reaction. His face turned quite red and he became very angry. In a furious tone of voice he responded, "Doesn't she believe God did anything when she was baptized as a baby? Just wait till I see her." I was stunned that something that I thought was lovely and precious was regarded by him as wrong.

Peter's story

Peter told everyone that when he arrived on a healing retreat he had been full of anger and bitterness and with murderous intentions. His son, through no fault of his own, was facing bankruptcy because of being defrauded by a business partner. "This man," said Peter, "caused turmoil in our family. In his greed he caused utter chaos and was destroying us. I came here hating him and wanting to kill him." Peter, instead of being able to relax and enjoy his retirement years, was using his small pension to try to help pay off his son's debts.

> "I came here hating him and wanting to kill him."

During the retreat Peter was able to face and deal with the strong emotions he was feeling. He was able to forgive the man. In a time of public testimony he told us all, "I now have peace that I never thought possible. I now know that I could walk up to the person who did this evil thing to my son and say, 'I forgive you.' That is how much God has worked in my life. All I want now is for God to use me. I thank God for the work He has done in me."

These snippets, from the lives of people we have encountered over the years, give a glimpse of some of the ways people try to handle their anger. Some have expressed their unrighteous anger. Some have buried their anger along with their hurt and pain. Others have expressed their anger in harmful and destructive ways.

> They have learned how to move forward into the future without being chained to the events of the past.

A very few have learned to handle their anger in godly ways. They have learned how to identify the causes of their anger and to recognize that their feelings of anger for what has happened are God-given and appropriate. They have learned how to express their emotions in a rightful way. They have learned how to release forgiveness to those who have hurt them. They have learned how to move forward into the future without being chained to the events of the past.

What Is Anger?

What is anger? We cannot look at the answer to this question without first answering the question "Who are we?" Many people struggle with the expression of anger in wrongful ways because they have little understanding of who they are, and how God created them to operate. Unless we understand how our emotions are supposed to function, we will have difficulty in expressing them and reacting to them in a godly way.

Who are we?

We have all been brought up in an increasingly secular and atheistic world, a world which has attempted to brainwash us into believing that we are the product of evolutionary chance. The Bible in marked contrast tells us that we are created beings, made in the image of God to fulfill the purposes of God.

In Genesis 2:7 we read how God took the dust of the earth, formed it into the first human being, breathed into him the breath of life and man became a living being. Why is this in the Bible? One reason is because it tells us that we are more than just physical beings. It says that we have both a visible material part and also an invisible spiritual part.

The invisible part of our being is referred to in the Old Testament using words such as "heart," "soul" and "spirit." These words are often used interchangeably. In the New Testament, however, a distinction is drawn between our soul and spirit. Paul refers to us being whole in body, soul and spirit (1 Thessalonians 5:23) and the writer to the Hebrews talks about the word of God being able to divide between soul and spirit (Hebrews 4:12). In summary, therefore, we can say that we are created and have three dimensions to our creation – body, soul and spirit.

> "[God] *knit me together in my mother's womb.*"
> (Psalm 139:13)

This miracle of creation that we read about in the Book of Genesis is repeated with each new baby that is conceived. The new baby's physical attributes come to him or her from the parents' genes, but this baby is more than just a physical being. In the wonderful words of Psalm 139 David says with assurance, "[God] *knit me together in my mother's womb*" (v. 13). God was involved in forming your spirit, soul and body and growing them into that unique individual which is you.

- **The body** is the physical part. It is the skin, bones, muscles, sinews, nervous system, senses, brain and other physical organs which are material and visible.
- **The soul** consists of the mind, the will and the emotions.
  - *The mind* is the part with which we think, analyze and process the information received through our senses and our spirit.
  - *The will* enables us to make choices.
  - *The emotions* are the place where we register and process our internal feelings.

- **The spirit** is that innermost part of our being. It is that
part of us that contains our identity, our creativity, our
conscience, and through which we relate to God. It is
that part of us that imparts life to our whole being and
which is eternal and will never die.

Our emotions

Our emotions are the inner reactions or feelings that we have
to the circumstances (real or perceived) happening around us.
They are a measure of how we feel about ourselves and our
environment. We enjoy the good positive feelings we have
when things are going well. We don't like the unpleasant
feelings we experience when things are not going well. It can
be difficult for us to put into words exactly what we are feeling,
and especially as, at any one time, we may be experiencing a
mixture of emotions.

One of the reasons God gave us emotions was that He
wanted us to enjoy life. If we had no feelings about the things
we do in life, there wouldn't be any incentive to do anything
that we enjoy. Our emotions can be a motivating force in
our lives. Grief and sadness about the misfortunes of others
can cause us to want to reach out and help them. Anger
at injustice can be a motivating force driving us to alleviate the
injustice.

> Anger at injustice can be a motivating force
> driving us to alleviate the injustice.

We need to acknowledge that our emotions are God given.
They are a part of our very being. God has emotions, and
we have been made in His image. The Bible describes Him as
having a wide range of emotions. He grieves, He loves, He
rejoices with singing, and He is angered. Jesus most certainly

had emotions and expressed them. As Christians we are all in a process of being made more and more like Jesus. We know also that the Holy Spirit has emotions because the Bible warns us not to grieve Him (Ephesians 4:30).

We should be able to experience a range of emotions. What we feel will be appropriate to the circumstances if our emotions are working properly. For example, you may feel pleased to hear some good news about an acquaintance that you hardly know, feel quite happy if the person is your friend, but feel excited and ecstatic if it is a close family member. Your emotional response varies appropriately with the circumstances.

On the other hand, if your emotional response to some event is disproportionate, it is an indication that some inner healing may be required. You might feel no emotional response to an event that will have a significant impact on your life, or you might have an over-the-top reaction to some minor incident. Reactions like these show that the emotions are not working as they should. They are an indicator that there is almost certainly a need for God's healing.

Our emotions do not operate independently of the rest of our being but are influenced by our memories and thoughts. A situation that you find yourself in today may bring back memories of events from the past, together with your emotions and feelings about that past event. Your child, for example, tells you that she was picked on at school by her friends. You rightfully feel angry about this, but the intensity of your anger might be much deeper if you too had been bullied when you were at school.

Another way in which our emotions are affected by our minds and thoughts is this: we tend to analyze the present situation in our minds and project or anticipate the future outcome. If we anticipate a good outcome our feelings will be positive and we may feel excited, happy or joyful. If we anticipate uncertain or bad outcomes our feelings may be fear, worry or anxiety. If your boss, for example, asks you to step into his office for a moment, you might assume that he is going to be critical of your work. You respond in your emotions and you start to begin to feel anxious or afraid before he has even said what he wants to talk about.

> The emotional response we feel is often expressed through the rest of our being.

The emotional response we feel is often expressed through the rest of our being. If we are happy our eyes may sparkle, there will be a smile on our faces and we may be full of energy. If we are sad and depressed our face may be downcast, our eyes may fill with tears and we may feel lethargic. If we are fearful we may experience physical pain in our chest or head, our rate of breathing may increase or our bodies may shake uncontrollably. Your body reflects your emotional state.

Our emotions can change very quickly in response to changed circumstances. We can be feeling very calm and peaceful when suddenly the fire alarm sounds. Immediately we may feel fearful and anxious. We can be feeling down and depressed when we hear the exciting news that a long-lost relative has left us a lot of money in his will. Instantaneously our mood changes and the depression lifts. It doesn't take long for some emotional changes to happen.

The emotion of anger

Anger is one of the many emotions that we may experience in relation to the situations around us. It is a feeling of disapproval, dislike or opposition towards what is happening to us. The Chambers Dictionary defines it as "hot displeasure provoked by some action, incident or situation often involving hostility and a desire for retaliation."

There are many different English words that we could use to try and describe the intensity of anger. These include: annoyed, upset, irritated, exasperated, infuriated, frustrated, enraged, furious, cross, mad, aggressive, hostile and incensed. The intensity of anger is very subjective. Something that you find only mildly irritating may cause someone else to go into a deep rage.

The intensity of our anger is very subjective.

Because of the negative connotations of the word "anger," many people choose not to use this word when talking about their emotional feelings. They might say "I feel annoyed" or "I feel frustrated" but inside they are really seething with anger, whether they are aware of it or not. In fact it is possible to be so out of touch with emotions that some people don't think that they have any feelings at all, although it can be obvious from their body posture and language that they are very angry.

In writing about anger in his book *Right Relationships* Tom Marshall says, "One of the problems is that our language has no way of distinguishing between anger as a feeling and anger as a behaviour, but the distinction is of crucial importance."[1] We may fail to recognize the difference between anger as a feeling and anger as behavior. We may believe that it is only the behavior which should be called anger. In other words, we only admit or acknowledge that we are angry when we lash out in acts of violence against inanimate objects or others.

I might claim "I wasn't angry" but perhaps what I really mean is that I didn't slam the door, punch the wall or throw something at the person with whom I felt angry. The truth is that I did feel angry although I did not turn that feeling of anger into a physical display. It is good to own our feelings even if we don't like them. When we own them, we can start dealing with them, and responding to them in godly ways.

One of the keys to dealing with anger is to recognize the distinction between feelings of anger on the one hand and angry behavior on the other. Feelings of anger can be righteous. We need to determine whether our feelings of anger are righteous and then take responsibility for the behavior that comes out of these feelings.

Righteous and unrighteous anger

Because anger is often associated with ungodly behavior, many Christians have developed a belief that all anger is somehow wrong or sinful. Lack of teaching on this subject may have reinforced this belief. When they feel angry many people deny it or suppress it. Others know they are angry but feel guilty about it, allowing the enemy to bring them under condemnation.

> To feel angry is not always wrong.

The assumption they are making is that all anger is ungodly or unrighteous. However, because our emotions are God given, and because God experiences anger, this assumption that all anger is ungodly has to be wrong. **To feel angry is not always wrong.** In fact, if we don't sometimes feel angry there is something wrong with us.

Here are some important questions to ask yourself when you are feeling angry:

- Is it OK to feel angry about this situation?
- Is my anger a righteous anger?
- Have I somehow got a distorted picture of what is going on?
- Am I allowing past events in my life to influence my feelings about current situations?

The real test of whether our feelings of anger are righteous is whether God shares our anger. If we have been sinned against, God is angry about that sin. If we also feel angry about it, then our feelings of anger are righteous. Many times in ministry we have had to tell people that God is angry that they were abused or controlled by others.

On the other hand, if we feel angry because someone has not responded the way we wanted them to, our anger is probably unrighteous. If we feel angry with the traffic warden who is only doing his job or the policeman who has caught us speeding, our anger is almost certainly unrighteous.

> She was angry with God for allowing it to happen.

Often our anger can be a mixture of righteous and unrighteous anger. Katie was a victim of childhood sexual abuse and full of anger. She was righteously angry about what had happened to her. She was righteously angry that her mum had disbelieved her story when she tried to tell her what her stepfather was doing. However, part of her anger was directed towards God. She was angry with God for allowing it to happen and was blaming Him for what had happened to her. Instead of being righteously angry with Satan, her anger had become unrighteous and directed against God.

We also need to recognize that we can have feelings of righteous anger but could be acting out of these in unrighteous ways. Joyce had cause for righteous anger about the things that had happened to her. Expressing this anger in violent outbursts at house group or vandalizing the church floral displays was obviously sinful. The feelings of righteous anger do not justify the unrighteous behavior. The Bible says, *"In your anger do not sin"* (Ephesians 4:26).

One man told us that in an angry confrontation with a work colleague he smashed a chair. As we talked through the incident it was apparent that his feelings of anger may have been righteous but his actions were not. He had great difficulty in accepting this. The person he was angry with was so surprised by the outburst of anger that he subsequently changed his behavior. Even though the outcome apparently appeared good, it was achieved through ungodly means and there was a need to confess and repent of this ungodly behavior.

Our feelings of anger can, therefore, be righteous or unrighteous and the behavior driven by our feelings can also be righteous or unrighteous. In the next chapter we will look at some of the reasons why we may feel angry.

Note

1. Sovereign World, 1989.

Why Am I So Angry?

Where does the powerful emotion of anger come from? What things happen to me and around me that stir up my angry feelings, which then seem to override all other emotions? In this chapter we are going to explore some of the root causes behind anger. As we go through these different causes of anger, you may like to ask yourself each time:

- Has this ever happened to me?
- If so, did it make me angry?
- How did I respond?

Injustice

Each one of us has an inbuilt sense of what is right and wrong. It is as if we instinctively know when something unfair or unjust has happened. The response we have to injustice will include anger.

In 2 Samuel 12 we read how the prophet Nathan confronts David about his sin. He does this by telling a story in which a wealthy man prepares a meal for a visiting traveler. Instead of providing the feast from his abundant riches, he takes the only lamb of a poor man and has that slaughtered instead. David's reaction is to be filled with anger at the injustice of what the rich man had done, and Nathan goes on to show David that he had behaved in the same way.

> David burned with anger against the man and
> said to Nathan, "As surely as the LORD lives,
> the man who did this deserves to die!"
> (2 Samuel 12:5)

It is natural to feel angry at injustices done to ourselves. It might be the times you have been wrongly accused of something. Maybe someone slandered you by telling lies about you. Perhaps you were treated unfairly. Your brothers or sisters were shown favoritism. They were always given more than you or treated better than you.

What about punishment? When we are subject to unfair discipline or punishment we can feel a deep sense of injustice and anger. The same is true when we feel we have been deceived or cheated. Perhaps you have been cheated out of an inheritance that was rightfully yours or perhaps someone has not kept their word. George said that, as a young boy in school, his teacher promised to give a sweet, at the end of the day, to everyone who behaved themselves. He was on his best behavior all day so he felt really angry when at the end of the day the teacher declared that no one deserved a sweet.

Injustices done to others can make us angry too. When others are subjected to things that we would not want to have happen to us, we can react on the inside. What about injustices done to your children? When we hear of children being exploited and abused, anger arises within us. When we read in the newspapers of the indignities that people have had to endure in hospital through neglect and lack of care, we feel angry. When we see pictures on the television of the emaciated victims of the latest famine brought about through local tribal warfare we sense something of the injustice of their situation.

We can become incensed and angry when we see or hear of cruelty to pets and animals. Feelings can also be aroused because others neglect or damage the environment. Take a moment to consider the times when you have been the victim of injustice. How did you feel and how did you respond?

Betrayal

Have you ever been betrayed? Betrayal produces deep feelings of anger. It is painful when someone in whom you have placed your trust, betrays that trust. Betrayal comes in all shapes and sizes. It can be a broken confidence, something that you shared with a close friend only to discover that your secret became a subject of gossip. It could be the deep pain of discovering that your boyfriend is two-timing you, or that your marriage partner is having an adulterous affair.

Betrayal will be accompanied by much anger. There will be anger towards the betrayer. There may be anger towards any third party involved. There is likely to be anger towards yourself: "How could I have been so stupid as to let this happen?"

> *They were filled with grief and fury,*
> *because Shechem had done a disgraceful thing...*
> (Genesis 34:7)

There is an example of this kind of anger in the Bible. In Genesis 34 we read how the Shechemites violated Dinah, the daughter of Jacob, after Jacob had settled in the land he purchased from them. Jacob's sons were filled with grief and fury because they felt that the Shechemites had betrayed the trust that had been put in them. In their fury they took revenge and killed all the men of Shechem.

Another type of betrayal is most kinds of physical, emotional, spiritual or sexual abuse. It is a violation of our being, usually by people with authority over us. Within our spirit we know this should not have happened. There will be anger that it has happened. There may well be anger towards those who should have protected us from the abuse. There can be anger towards the people who did not believe us when we tried to tell them what was going on. Like the young girl who tried to tell her mother what had happened when she was left alone with her stepfather, only to be told, "You wicked child, how dare you say such things?" This is betrayal by someone who ought to have been her protection.

Where there has been abuse there is usually a distorted picture of what God is like and often there will be anger against Him. The enemy will seek to undermine our trust in God by tormenting us with questions such as: Why did He let it happen? Why didn't He do something to stop it? Why me?

There can be anger against ourselves for allowing the abuse to continue. Abused children usually try to rationalize what has happened and conclude that somehow it was their fault – that they should have stopped it happening. This false guilt and anger towards self may find an outward expression in self-harm.

Despite all the damage caused by abuse, God is able to bring healing. Sylvia gave this written testimony at the end of a healing retreat at Ellel Grange:

> "I have spent most of my life dominated by fear and anger, and unable to relate properly to other people. I was constantly struggling with anger, self-pity, rejection and the inability to really know God. I arrived here apprehensive, bound up and angry, but God began to work from the first ministry session. Although the process was difficult and extremely painful I never once felt threatened or rejected. Because of this I was able to

allow God to touch memories of sexual abuse that had been buried all my life. They were exposed, dealt with and healed."

Perhaps you might like to consider at this point whether you have been betrayed in some way.

Failure

Failure is often a root cause of anger. It might be the failure of others to meet our expectations. Their failure to perform as we would wish can leave us bitter, resentful and angry. When the expectation we have of others is unrealistic, the anger that arises when they fail us will be unrighteous.

> *But Naaman went away angry and said, "I thought that he would surely come out to me and stand and call on the name of the LORD his God, wave his hand over the spot and cure me of my leprosy."*
> (2 Kings 5:11)

When Naaman was seeking healing for his leprosy, Elisha did not behave the way Naaman thought he should behave. You can read this story in 2 Kings 5. Instead of going out to meet this important dignitary, Elisha had merely sent a servant with a message telling Naaman to go and wash himself in the river. Naaman's response was one of indignation. He was furious that Elisha had not treated him with the respect he thought he deserved.

We, too, can feel angry because others have not treated us in the way we wanted them to. We can feel annoyed that the pastor didn't visit us when we were ill or didn't do what we wanted. We can feel angry with the doctor who kept us waiting while he or she attended to another patient.

We can feel angry with spouses because they don't live up to the unrealistic expectation we had created in our minds. A woman may marry the man of her dreams and then discover they both come home from work tired, but he doesn't want to share the household chores. She discovers his irritating habits of untidiness and making a mess which is always left for her to clean up. His selfishness causes her to feel angry. Or maybe a man marries "Miss Right" and then finds out she's secretly spending money on luxuries they can't afford and running up debts. Her failure to live up to his expectation may leave him feeling resentful and angry.

Sometimes we fail to meet the expectations we place upon ourselves. We feel disappointed that we have let ourselves and others down. Sometimes out of fear of being rejected by others we set impossibly high standards of achievement for ourselves. We can set higher standards for ourselves than we would set for others. By striving to perform we hope to be accepted and, when we fail, we become angry with ourselves.

When we fail we can start to reject ourselves. We may even think we deserve to be punished and in some cases may even express that through self-harming. In extreme cases we may even entertain suicidal thoughts and attempt to take our own life. Such thoughts and actions are ultimately an expression of anger against ourselves.

Sometimes, it is the failure of God to act in the way we want Him to act, that is the root of our anger. Over the years, many people who have come for ministry have found they were harboring anger towards God, deep on the inside. In their heart they may think, "God is Sovereign and should have done something," or "If God really cares about me, why am I still single?" or "Where were You, God, when I was being abused?"

We so easily lose sight of the fact that we are in a spiritual battle. We forget that there is an enemy of our souls who delights in the bad things that happen to us. We forget that each person has been given free will and that God doesn't override that free will even when it is exercised to hurt and harm others. We can so easily forget that God has demonstrated how much He loves and cares for us by what happened at Calvary. We can become bitter and angry with God in our hearts if we lose sight of all these things.

When has failure made you angry? Other people's failure? Your own failure? How have you responded?

Affronts to our personal values

Each individual holds personal belief systems and values. These develop through the influence of other people, environmental factors and our individual experiences of life. We can find it difficult to understand why anyone would have different values from our own. We sometimes think rather arrogantly that others should share our views and opinions. We are right, we tell ourselves, and we pray that God will give others the same revelation!

> *His disciples remembered that it is written:*
> *"Zeal for your house will consume me."*
> (John 2:17)

When others disagree with us or don't value things in the way we do, we can feel angry. It might be, for example, when we see a television program expressing atheistic and secular views about evolution and creation. It could equally be a so-called "Christian theologian" expounding his deceptive and heretical views about the person of Jesus.

We may know people who get upset and angry if others do not agree that the football team they support is the best in the league, or that the political party they adhere to is the only one capable of running the country.

Anyone who has been to an annual church meeting will know how strongly some folk feel about the songs that should be sung in church, or the way communion should be served. Discussion and debate on such issues can lead to very angry outbursts as individuals try to impose their viewpoint on others. The vicar in Liz's story in chapter 1, who was angry that one of his congregation wanted to undergo full immersion baptism, was obviously facing a challenge to one of his personal values.

When we feel angry in this way we need to take some time to stop and reflect. Ask the questions: Does God feel angry about this? Is this an issue that I feel so strongly about that it is worth dying for? We need, also, to try and see things from the perspective of others, and realize that others, too, may feel strongly about issues, but not necessarily agree with our views.

You might like to think about whether you have felt angry because others did not share your values. Perhaps you need to consider how strongly you feel about these values and whether they are godly ones.

Frustration

Frustration is a major trigger to angry feelings and angry behavior. All of us feel a certain amount of frustration whenever someone, or something, seems to block our goals. At times we can wonder, "Why can't everyone else see the importance of what I am trying to do or to achieve?"

We may get angry at others for not co-operating with us and can even presume, quite erroneously, that they are deliberately trying to hinder us. Some people blame the devil, for example getting angry when the photocopier jams, calling it a spiritual attack every time. We can even get angry with God for not miraculously intervening so that we can quickly accomplish the tasks we have set ourselves.

If you are a doer and task-orientated person you can quickly get restless and irritated when progress towards your goal is blocked. You may say to yourself, "Why is it that I always get in the supermarket check-out queue that moves at a snail's pace or always get stuck behind the car that wants to turn while all the other traffic overtakes me on the inside?"

> *So Ahab went home, sullen and angry because*
> *of what Naboth the Jezreelite had said . . .*
> *He lay on his bed sulking and refused to eat.*
> (1 Kings 21:4)

In 1 Kings 21 we read how Ahab was frustrated and angry when his goals were blocked. When he was not able to buy Naboth's vineyard he lay on his bed and sulked. The final outcome was that Jezebel had Naboth murdered so that Ahab could have his own way.

It is very easy for us to allow feelings of frustration and impatience to lead us into unrighteous thoughts and behavior. For example, we can kick or punch the drink dispenser that has swallowed our money, but refuses to release the can of cold drink that we paid for.

The amount of frustration we feel depends on the importance we place on reaching our goals and to some extent on our personality type. Task-orientated people are often impatient and need to be aware of how quickly they can become frustrated and how easily those feelings of frustration can lead to ungodly behavior.

If you are task orientated and you are focusing very intensely on the particular task you are seeking to accomplish, what may be minor irritations to others may feel like major frustrations to you. Of course the depth of feeling will also depend on the duration of the circumstances blocking your goals. To take a relatively minor problem, for example, the longer you are stuck in the traffic jam the more frustrated and angry you are likely to feel.

When our longer-term goals in life are blocked, such as our desire to be married or to have a child, we also experience frustration. The danger of such frustrations is that we can end up feeling resentful and bitter towards others or God. When facing such long-term frustrations we need to try and submit our desires and goals to God and try to avoid them becoming the controlling focus of our lives.

Ask yourself whether you have a low tolerance level of frustration when your goals are blocked. Are you aware of lashing out at others or of becoming bitter with God because of your frustration?

Rejection

Another very common cause of anger is rejection. God created us as relational beings and each one of us has an inborn desire to feel accepted and valued as a person. We need to be valued for who we are and not for what we do. When this need for acceptance is not met there is hurt and pain. Often we feel angry because these needs are not being met.

It is natural to feel angry when you are undervalued as a person. If a parent always insists that the house is immaculately clean and tidy and children are not allowed to play in case they make a mess, a message is given that the child is less important than a tidy house.

If a husband leaves his dirty clothes lying around the bedroom for his wife to pick up, his wife will feel unappreciated and taken for granted. Inside she may well feel angry. If you are bypassed for a job or promotion at work feelings of anger may arise. This will be especially so if you consider the job has been given to someone less qualified and less competent than yourself.

Equally if you are criticized and put down and never

affirmed for what you do, you will feel angry because criticism is a form of rejection. If this is done in front of others you may feel humiliation and shame. There can even be more anger because your weaknesses and moral failures have been made public.

When we are rejected we experience many emotions. These may include shame, confusion and anger.

When we feel rejected we experience a range of emotions. Obviously we feel pain and sadness. There can be loneliness and despair, and often there will be confusion and anger. The good news is that Jesus can break into our lives and bring healing. Pam wrote the following:

> "My God has been so kind and gentle to me. He has held me in His arms all weekend. My parents divorced when I was thirteen, resulting in deep rejection, pain, anger, confusion and self-rejection in my life. God has shown me His deep faithful love and has lifted off these burdens."

Unhealed hurts

The anger we feel because of current circumstances often has its true root in the past. Present situations can trigger into the hurt, pain and anger that we suppressed in the past. We have already looked at how rejection or the failure of others can cause anger. If the rejection was in our childhood, it is highly probable that we were not given the opportunity to work through and resolve the anger we felt at that time.

This past anger may be, for example, that no one protected us from the bullying and ridicule of our classroom peers. It could be anger at our parents for their lack of protection which allowed us to be abused. It could, for example, be like the anger

Mary felt at having to make a choice about which parent she would live with when she loved both of them and did not want them to divorce.

It might be that the unresolved issues of the past feed our anger. We can be very good at storing up our hurt and anger. Ephesians 4:26 tells us not to let the sun go down on our anger but we can struggle to do that. If your spouse or friend, for example, does something that upsets you, do you talk it through and resolve your differences? Do you instead push it down and let it simmer until the next time you feel upset with him or her? The pain and anger from the past then reinforces what we are feeling in the present. The result is an emotional overreaction, which prevents the current issue from being resolved, so we just bury everything again and perpetuate the relationship problems.

If we fail to forgive and keep resentment and bitterness in our hearts it leads to an accumulation of anger. We may unrealistically be waiting for the person who has hurt us to acknowledge this fact.

You may like to ask yourself this question: Are there events in my past about which I still feel angry?

Behavioral patterns

Anger can become part of our behavioral pattern. We might never have been shown what to do with our emotions or we might have discovered how we can use our anger to get our needs met by others. As a result of poor parenting we may have learned that throwing a temper tantrum gets us what we want. We might copy the way we saw our parents manipulate each other with their anger.

We need to be careful that we don't justify this wrong use of our emotions by denying any responsibility for it and claiming it is our personality. Rather, we need to ask God to teach us new behavioral patterns. Some people have learnt to use their anger as a defense mechanism to try and stop other people getting too close to their hurt and pain. Their tendency to get angry is a threat to others which causes everyone to keep their distance.

When confronted Uzziah became angry.

We find King Uzziah behaving like this in 2 Chronicles 26:16–19. He became full of pride and went into the Temple to burn incense. This was contrary to the Law which only permitted the descendants of Aaron to carry out this task. When the priests confronted Uzziah about his actions he became angry. He used his anger to try and protect himself from confrontation.

Ask yourself:

- Is this something I have learned to do?
- Do I use my anger to control others and get my own way?

These, then, are just some of the reasons why we get angry. In the next chapter we will look at what the Bible has to say about God's anger. You may find this surprising.

CHAPTER

What Does the Bible Say about Anger?

4

Have you ever thought of God as having emotions? Do you feel that God's love is incompatible with anger? It isn't. We are made in the image of God and He has emotions like we do. What makes Him angry?

The anger of God

The anger of God can be described as the emotional response of God when His instructions are ignored or when His holiness or righteousness is brought into question. We find God's anger being kindled by idolatry. In passages such as Deuteronomy 32:16–31 we read that God's jealousy and anger were aroused when the Israelites worshiped the idols of foreign religions. It is an affront to God's holiness and righteousness when anything but God has the place of prominence in our lives.

> *Do not follow other gods . . .*
> *for the LORD your God . . . is a jealous God*
> *and his anger will burn against you . . .*
> (Deuteronomy 6:14–15)

You may not be in a false religion, and be worshiping in a Hindu or Buddhist temple, but you can still have idols in your hearts. Things such as your car, house, money, position, spouse, children or status may be more important to you than God. Inviting Jesus to be Lord over every part of your life is an important step in moving forward into healing and wholeness.

The Bible tells us that God's anger is aroused by disobedience and sinfulness. When the Israelites went into the Promised Land they were specifically told not to take for themselves the idols of the people living in the land. We see in Joshua chapter 7 how Achan disobeyed this instruction. As a result the Israelites' enemies started to be victorious over them until this disobedience was uncovered and dealt with.

> *But the Israelites acted unfaithfully in regard*
> *to the devoted things; Achan ... took some of them.*
> *So the Lord's anger burned against Israel.*
> (Joshua 7:1)

As parents we set boundaries for our children. We tell them not to go too near an open fire or not to touch the pan of boiling water. We tell them not to play in the street or not to cross the road without carefully checking whether there are any cars coming. We set these boundaries to protect our children because we love them and care for them. When they disobey we feel anxiety, concern, frustration and anger. These feelings generally arise, not just because our authority has been challenged, but because we are aware of the danger and consequences that our children have exposed themselves to by their disobedience.

It is important for us to recognize that God experiences anger in a similar way. God has established safe boundaries within which we should operate. Summarized within the

Ten Commandments (Exodus 20:1–17), they give us safe boundaries within which to relate to God and to one another. In our disobedience to God, we move ourselves out of the boundaries of protection that God established for us, and open ourselves up to the consequences, which may include the attack of the enemy in our lives. (We will explore this more fully in a later chapter.) God, as a loving Father, feels exasperated and angry when those whom He has created ignore these protective boundaries, just as we do when our children ignore the boundaries we set for them.

> But Moses said, "O Lord, please send someone
> else to do it." Then the Lord's anger
> burned against Moses . . .
> (Exodus 4:13–14)

God's anger was aroused by the actions of individuals as well as the corporate actions of nations. In Exodus 4:14 we find Moses caused God to be angry when he was resisting the call God was putting on his life. God had already demonstrated in miraculous ways that He was with Moses, but Moses replied, "Please send someone else." I wonder if God still gets a bit frustrated when you or I hear clearly from God, yet resist what He is saying to us.

The corporate actions of the nation of Israel often stirred God to anger. In the Book of Numbers chapter 25 we are told how the Israelites began to indulge in sexual immorality with the Moabite women, which led them into worshiping their false gods. As a consequence we read that *"the Lord's anger burned against them"* (Numbers 25:3). Have you ever asked yourself whether God's anger may be burning against parts of His Church for remaining silent about sexual behavior which is clearly outside of God's will? God knows how harmful such behavior is to us.

The wrath of God

The Bible talks about the anger of God and it also talks about the wrath of God. The wrath of God refers to acts of righteous judgment and punishment initiated by God. Deuteronomy 29:22–28 clearly indicates that desolation of the land, and the uprooting of the Israelites from it, was an outpouring of God's wrath, because of their rejection of God. His righteous judgment removed them all, and only those who still wanted to follow Him returned later. So the land was cleansed. Otherwise they would have fallen away from Him completely.

> *In furious anger and in great wrath*
> *the LORD uprooted them from their land and*
> *thrust them into another land, as it is now.*
> (Deuteronomy 29:28)

The wrath of God can be considered as the execution of God's judgment upon the actions of those who have rejected Him and who have committed all kinds of evil as a result (Revelation 14:19; 16:1 and 19:15). The Bible presents the wrath of God as being motivated by God's anger. Yet this wrath is tempered by His mercy and His forgiveness. This is well brought out in Psalm 78:38 where we read,

> *Yet he was merciful;*
> *he forgave their iniquities*
> *and did not destroy them.*
> *Time after time he restrained his anger*
> *and did not stir up his full wrath.*

As we have already discussed, it is important that we differentiate between anger as a feeling, and the behavior which is the outward expression of these feelings. The Bible tells us that God is slow to anger. This does not mean that God does not immediately feel angry when He sees people being hurt or abused by others, but rather that He doesn't immediately act out of that anger, by pouring out His wrath on those who are being sinful. God, in His mercy and compassion, does not always execute His judgment on sin immediately.

> *The LORD is compassionate and gracious,*
> *slow to anger, abounding in love.*
> (Psalm 103:8)

When we are sinned against our human nature wants God to act quickly and mete out vengeance on our behalf. When this doesn't happen some people direct their anger towards God. Steve, who had been badly bullied at school, wanted to know where God was when he was being bullied. We suggested he asked God to show him. We paused for a few moments and then he said, "God has just given me a picture. I was being punched in the face by this bully but Jesus was standing between me and the bully. Each time I was punched Jesus too was being punched." This picture helped Steve realize that God identified with his hurt and pain. It brought home to him the truth, that the things that hurt him also hurt God. This picture of Jesus being punched too gave Steve new understanding of the verse about Jesus:

> *He was despised and rejected by men,*
> *a man of sorrows, and familiar with suffering.*
>
>   (Isaiah 53:3)

God's wrath is a necessary part of bringing about justice and punishment for wrongdoing in the moral universe He has created. There must be a consequence for evil doing. Yet God's love means He longs to show mercy and forgiveness of sins, which is why He waits so patiently for men and women to repent and come into a relationship with Him. He is full of compassion and feels the pain with us as we suffer at the hands of those who hurt us.

The anger of man

The Bible not only talks about the anger of God and the wrath of God, but also has a lot to say about our anger and what we should do or not do with it. Some of the key teachings and related Scripture passages are as follows:

1. Be slow to anger for it is a foolish man who lives on anger

- *A fool shows his annoyance at once,*
    but a prudent man overlooks an insult.

    (Proverbs 12:16)

- *A patient man has great understanding,*
    but a quick-tempered man displays folly.

    (Proverbs 14:29)

- *A hot-tempered man stirs up dissension,*
    but a patient man calms a quarrel.

    (Proverbs 15:18)

- *Better a patient man than a warrior,*
    a man who controls his temper than
        one who takes a city.

    (Proverbs 16:32)

- *The discretion of a man makes him slow to anger,*
    And his glory is to overlook a transgression.

    (Proverbs 19:11 NKJV)

- *My dear brothers, take note of this: Everyone should be quick to listen, slow to speak and slow to become angry.*

(James 1:19)

2. Anger causes strife and contention

- *A hot-tempered man must pay the penalty;*
  if you rescue him, you will have to do it again.

(Proverbs 19:19)

- *Better to live in a desert*
  than with a quarrelsome and ill-tempered wife.

(Proverbs 21:19)

- *Like a city whose walls are broken down*
  is a man who lacks self-control.

(Proverbs 25:28)

- *An angry man stirs up dissension,*
  and a hot-tempered one commits many sins.

(Proverbs 29:22)

3. Anger is stirred up by harsh words and hence it is advisable not to be friends with someone who is controlled by anger

- *A gentle answer turns away wrath,*
  but a harsh word stirs up anger.

(Proverbs 15:1)

- *Do not make friends with a hot-tempered man,*
  do not associate with one easily angered ...

(Proverbs 22:24)

4. Unrighteous anger is sinful

- *"But I say to you that whoever is angry with his brother
  without a cause shall be in danger of the judgment."*
                                        (Matthew 5:22 NKJV)

5. We are encouraged to put away wrath and anger

- *Get rid of all bitterness, rage and anger, brawling and slander,
  along with every form of malice.*
                                        (Ephesians 4:31)

- *But now you must rid yourselves of all such things as these:
  anger, rage, malice, slander and filthy language from your lips.*
                                        (Colossians 3:8)

As we look at these biblical exhortations, we need again to ask
ourselves whether the Bible is talking about anger as a feeling,
or anger as a behavior. We do not think that these scriptures
are telling us that it is always wrong to *feel* angry. God feels
anger and as we are made in His image, something would be
amiss if we didn't sometimes feel angry. These scriptures are a
warning to us about what we should not *do* as a result of our
feelings.

The Bible's teaching on anger is summarized in a challenging
way in Ephesians 4:26–27 where Paul quotes from Psalm 4:4:

*"In your anger do not sin": Do not let the sun go down while
you are still angry, and do not give the devil a foothold.*

As we have already explored, anger in itself is not the sin issue.
Paul here is exhorting us to be careful that our emotion of anger
does not lead to sinful behavior. He appears to be recognizing
the difference between anger as a feeling and anger as an
ungodly action. When we are provoked by others, or feel that

we are being frustrated in meeting our goals, we need to be careful how we express these feelings.

> *"In your anger do not sin":*
> *Do not let the sun go down while you are still angry,*
> *and do not give the devil a foothold.*
> (Ephesians 4:26–27)

Paul's words in Ephesians 4 about not sinning when you feel angry, can be seen as a commentary on the Genesis 4 story of the murder of Abel by his brother Cain. Cain was angry because his sacrifice was less acceptable to God than his brother's. The Bible is unclear as to why that was so, but we suspect one thing which made the sacrifice unacceptable was the heart attitude. God warns Cain that *"sin is crouching at your door."* Cain ignored that warning and his inward anger was expressed in the murdering of his brother. Cain opened the door to the enemy and gave him a foothold. He didn't deal with his feeling of anger and there were dire consequences.

> *Then the LORD said to Cain, "Why are you angry?*
> *Why is your face downcast?"*
> (Genesis 4:6)

Paul encourages us to deal with our emotions and not dwell upon them or bury them. If my wife Liz and I have had a disagreement or argument we can both easily withdraw and become silent towards each other. In our minds we justify our own actions and opinions. We tell ourselves that our spouse is the one who is wrong and unreasonable. We open the door to self-pity, resentment, bitterness and even feelings of unrighteous anger towards one another. When we do this the enemy becomes the winner and we are the losers.

In summary, therefore, the scriptural challenge for all of us as Christians is not to sin when we feel angry. In subsequent chapters we will be looking at ways in which we can avoid sinning and how we can deal with our feelings of anger in godly ways.

What Can I Learn from Jesus about Anger?

Our perfect role model in handling our anger is Jesus. What did Jesus teach about anger? Did Jesus experience feelings of anger and, if He did, how did He express those feelings?

Jesus came not only to redeem His fallen creation, but also to reveal the true nature of God. One of the ways He revealed God's true nature was by explaining truths about the Kingdom of God, through parables. In many of these stories, one of the central figures is clearly a picture of God. We ourselves can usually identify, sometimes to our embarrassment and discomfort, with one of the other characters in the story.

A king, provoked to anger

Jesus told a story about a king and an unmerciful servant (Matthew 18). The king wanted to settle all the accounts but one of the servants was unable to pay his great debt. When the servant begged for mercy and time to try and repay the money the king took pity on him and cancelled the whole debt. Sadly the servant did not show any mercy to a fellow servant who owed him some money. Even though this servant begged for time to repay the debt, he had him thrown into prison. The king was told about it and became very angry at the ungrateful servant who had refused to show mercy to a fellow worker. This servant, who had been released from the great debt that he was unable to repay, was unwilling to grant any mercy to his co-worker who owed him some money. In fact it would appear that he was unfairly angry with his fellow servant and treated him harshly. In a similar way the unresolved anger in our lives can cause us to behave without compassion towards others.

> *"In anger his master turned him over to the jailers."*
> (Matthew 18:34)

The ingratitude and hard-heartedness displayed by the unmerciful servant provoked the king to anger and to action. This parable teaches us how important it is that we are willing to forgive those that sin against us. If we are unwilling to forgive, we provoke the anger of God, who, in His great mercy, has already offered us forgiveness through the death of Jesus.

Can you identify with the unmerciful servant? Do you sometimes find it hard to forgive?

A king, provoked by lukewarmness

In the parable of the great banquet (Luke 14:16–24) Jesus tells the story of a king who prepares a great feast for his friends and neighbors. When he sends out the invitations, however, his invited guests make feeble excuses and do not attend. This response angers the king.

In the letter to the church of Laodicea, Jesus' anger towards lukewarmness is again expressed:

> *"So, because you are lukewarm – neither hot nor cold – I am about to spit you out of my mouth."*
>
> (Revelation 3:16)

Do we provoke God to anger when we find other things in life to be more important than the things that God has for us? In trying to fulfill our own desires do we miss the plans, purposes and destiny that God has for each one of us?

A father, slow to anger

In the story of the prodigal son, the younger of two sons asks his father for his inheritance (Luke 15:11–32). The son goes away and wastes all the money, but then decides to return home and say sorry. He doesn't expect to be received back into the family but is willing to become a servant to his father. The behavior of this young man's father tells us much about the nature of God. The father, who had many reasons to be angry with his son, instead shows him mercy and compassion. The father is waiting and watching for the young man's return. When he sees him returning home in disgrace he runs to meet him and throws his arms around him. If it were our son we would probably want to vent our anger. "What have you done with all your wealth? Why have you been so stupid? Don't you realize that you have made your mother sick with worry?"

> "His father saw him and
> was filled with compassion for him;
> he ran to his son, threw his arms around him
> and kissed him."
> (Luke 15:20)

The father in the story that Jesus told doesn't do any of these things. Under the Jewish Law he even had the right to have his rebellious son stoned to death (Deuteronomy 21:18–21). But the father does not behave in this way. He doesn't even wait to let the returning prodigal speak out his well-rehearsed apology. No – he runs to him and welcomes him home with open arms. Jesus, in this story, reaffirms the nature of God as being one who is *"slow to anger, abounding in love and faithfulness, maintaining love to thousands, and forgiving wickedness, rebellion and sin"* (Exodus 34:6–7).

How do you see God? Do you see God as someone who is quick to criticize and quick to punish or do you see Him as a compassionate, loving Father?

A brother's unrighteous anger

In the story of the prodigal son, it is not the father who reacts in anger but the young man's brother. This may have made many of those listening somewhat uncomfortable. They had been critical of Jesus for welcoming the people whom they had rejected as being sinners and outcasts. In their hearts they were angry, perhaps, that Jesus had not praised their religiosity and self-righteousness. In their hearts they were angry at the idea that God might not behave in the way they wanted Him to behave.

The attitude of the prodigal's brother is a challenge to our own hearts. Are you angry with God? Has God failed to behave the way you want Him to? Has God restrained His anger up until now and shown mercy to those who have hurt you? Do we trust that in the fullness of time, and with greater revelation and knowledge, we will be able to look back and see that all of God's actions have been just and righteous? Can we trust Him?

In the Sermon on the Mount Jesus teaches that ungodly expression of anger will be subject to judgment, just like murder. Feelings of anger can lead to murderous thoughts. Can you identify with the man described in chapter 1 who came on a healing retreat hating and ready to kill the man who had defrauded his son of all his wealth?

Jesus, angry with hypocrisy

Did Jesus get angry? He didn't sin but He did experience feelings of anger. In Mark 3:1–6 we read how Jesus went into the synagogue and healed the man with the shriveled hand. Some of the people there saw an opportunity to accuse Him of not keeping the Sabbath. Jesus was angry at the stubbornness of the people's hearts. They were far more interested in criticizing Jesus for breaking the Law (as they interpreted it) than praising God and rejoicing in the miraculous healing they had just witnessed.

> *He looked round at them in anger ...*
> *deeply distressed at their stubborn hearts ...*
> (Mark 3:5)

The Pharisees became so angry that they plotted to kill Jesus. Jesus, in turn, was outraged by their hypocrisy, and His feelings remind us of the anger of God described in Ezekiel chapter 34 towards the so-called "shepherds of Israel" who were failing to meet the needs of God's chosen people.

Jesus, indignant when we miss the heart of God

At times Jesus also felt frustrated or indignant at the behavior of the disciples. On one occasion (Mark 10:13–16) we read that Jesus was indignant with the disciples for trying to stop parents bringing children to Him to be blessed. It was not their hearts' intention which angered Jesus. Their desire, no doubt, was to try and protect their master from the demands of the crowds. Jesus' indignation stemmed from their lack of appreciation of how much Jesus wanted to bless the little children.

We wonder if we, too, often miss the heart of God. Could our well-intended religiosity ever stop us or others from intimately connecting with God? It's easy to do it. It is easy to criticize the disciples, but it's worth asking ourselves how often we, too, might be missing the heart of God.

Jesus, consumed with zeal for God

Indignation and zeal for the things of God motivated Jesus to action. All four gospels give an account of how Jesus drove the traders and moneylenders from the Temple. Many of the people visiting the Temple traveled long distances so it was impractical to bring the sacrificial animals with them. Others, no doubt, were artisans or craftsmen with no animals of their own. So they needed to purchase sacrifices to present in the Temple and their need had created a market in which unscrupulous traders were able to profit.

> *His disciples remembered that it is written,*
> *"Zeal for your house will consume me."*
> (John 2:17)

It is very likely that it was the way in which the pilgrims in the Temple were being cheated that angered Jesus. His feelings of anger motivated Him to action. He made a whip and drove the animals from the Temple and He overturned the tables of the moneylenders (John 2:12–17). It was zeal for the things of God that motivated the actions of Jesus.

Jesus' behavior in the Temple is a challenge to each one of us. Do we allow our feelings of anger to motivate us to godly action, or do we allow ourselves to be controlled by fear of man and end up in passivity? Are you sufficiently consumed by zeal for the things of God to pray this prayer? *"Lord Jesus, provoke me to anger at injustice and ungodliness and help me harness that anger to take action."*

In His teaching and in His behavior Jesus confirms that anger is an emotion experienced by both God and by ourselves. This anger can be godly and harnessed as a motivating force to do good, or it can be ungodly and uncontrolled leading to selfish and unrighteous actions. In the next chapter we will look at some of these ungodly ways in which we may have handled our anger in the past.

Anger ... How Have I Handled It?

So far we have been emphasizing the importance of distinguishing between anger as a feeling and anger as a behavior. With that understanding, we now need to ask ourselves, "What do I do, or what have I done in the past, with my feelings of anger?" It's an important question to ask because anger does not generally disappear into thin air.

Denial

One way some people deal with their anger is by denying it. They simply don't acknowledge that the feeling they are experiencing is anger. They might not recognize what they are feeling. It isn't always easy to recognize what a feeling is, especially if you have trained yourself to ignore or bury emotions. Or they may be reluctant to be honest about their feelings. They may give the angry feeling another name and say they feel frustrated or disappointed in the way someone has behaved towards them (not that they feel angry).

"Me! I'm not angry."

Others, despite their red faces, tightened fists and steam almost visibly coming out of their ears, might say through clenched teeth, "Me! I'm not angry." Why do they deny it? Perhaps they feel guilty for being angry or consider that acknowledging their true feelings is an admission that they have a character defect.

Suppression

Some people recognize that they are angry, but choose to suppress their anger, deliberately pushing it away.

Cathy described her suppression of anger this way:

> "I never heard my parents shouting or arguing. They never raised their voices. I found out that there were resentments but these were carefully concealed. One day I was shocked to overhear my dad swearing when he didn't know I could hear him. Emotions were controlled in my family so I learnt never to express them. I just felt them secretly and if I was ever angry I felt guilty about feeling that way and would go into self-rejection.
>
> Then I married and discovered my husband's family was completely different. His dad would feel provoked by criticism and would shout and express his anger. It felt catastrophic to me, but they amazingly always seemed to survive and recover after such explosions."

Why do people suppress their anger? For some it might be that they were punished as a child for expressing emotions. They may have been punished for crying or been threatened with, "If you don't stop crying I'll give you something to cry about." It might be that they were ridiculed for verbalizing how they felt. They may have been so dominated and controlled by others that passivity has taken over and they now feel unable or unwilling to confront situations which anger them.

Because of this insecurity they don't know what to do with their anger so they try to suppress it. They deliberately don't act out of their feelings and try to push them down and ignore them. In their minds, however, they entertain thoughts of disasters that they hope might befall the people who've angered them or what they would like to do to them! They might even rehearse in their minds what they would like to say to them.

> They get angry with themselves for not speaking
> out that they are angry.

Not surprisingly, they then feel guilty about having had such thoughts. They feel badly about themselves and may conclude that God must be angry with them for thinking such things. They might get angry with themselves for not having spoken out what they really felt.

Internalized anger

The suppression of anger can lead to self-harming, when the anger is expressed internally. A recent National Inquiry into self-harm concluded that as many as 10 per cent of children in Britain self-harm by cutting themselves with blades, deliberate bruising, head banging, taking overdoses of drugs or harming themselves in other ways. The report went on to say that the majority of self-harm cases remain hidden even from families.

Carol, a fourteen-year-old girl, reported how she left a family gathering, locked herself in a bathroom and cut herself on the back of her hand with a disposable razor. "Actually it was a real relief. I felt so calm from doing it," she said. "The family and everything else around me didn't matter. I'm a very shy and inward person and I would never take out my aggression on anyone else. So I was turning the anger on to myself. Part of this was turning pain in my mind to something physical so that I could deal with it, focus my attention on that rather than what was going on in my mind."

The ultimate in self-harming is to take one's own life. Many of the people that we minister to admit to having had suicidal thoughts during their life. In nearly all cases there has been deep rejection and usually suppressed anger at what others have done to them.

Passive aggression

Some people handle their anger through what is termed "passive aggression." They are often people who feel aggrieved. They see themselves as victims of some sort of injustice. They may feel angry at being put down, bypassed, or their opinions and ideas being ignored and rejected.

They are not the type to erupt suddenly, but they don't say how they feel either. Instead, they develop resentful attitudes, and may become uncooperative, uncommunicative and unhelpful. They stop being team players and become more self-centered. Because they feel angry they tend towards rebellion and may turn up late for meetings or show a lack of respect for those in authority. They are often critical and grumble.

> Because they communicate badly,
> no one knows the root cause of the problem.

These changed behavior patterns may happen gradually over a period of time. Because they communicate badly, no one knows the root cause of the problem. Such passive aggression needs to be challenged and confronted. It is important to show these people how their behavior is affecting others and causing breakdowns in relationships.

Verbal aggression

Most people, when they feel angry, give vent to their feelings through a verbal outburst which is generally subjective and often illogical. Their emotions take over like a volcano erupting inside of them. They raise their voices and the words often just pour out of them, sometimes punctuated with bad language and swearing.

> "Look what you've made me do now."

At times like this the words spoken out are often accusatory and damaging to others. "Look what you've made me do now"; "You don't care how I feel"; "I thought you were a Christian"; "You make me feel unloved"; "You always ruin everything"; "You never do your share"; "You don't understand how hard I have to work"; "You make me angry."

These verbal outbursts are often fuelled by the emotions and memories of past issues that have not been resolved, as if they have been stuffed down and stored in a rucksack. A wife may still be angry about the times her husband has got drunk and embarrassed her in front of friends. A husband may still be angry that his wife laughed at his secret fears and told her parents. A mother may still be angry that her son swore at her and kicked a hole in the door last week.

In such arguments most of us trawl our memories for any evidence that we can use to support our current feelings of anger, bitterness and resentment towards the person whom we perceive has hurt us. Inevitably those on the receiving end, now hurt and angry about the accusations being brought, will retaliate and start unpacking stored-up memories from their own rucksack as well. A small skirmish or battle thus quickly develops into a war.

Verbal aggression can also take the form of a cold and calculated onslaught which can be more damaging than the sudden short-lived eruption. Speech may be slow but delivered with venom. The words are spiteful and hurtful and almost always accusatory. Like a missile with a time-delayed fuse they have the ability to penetrate deep into the recipient's spirit where they explode with devastating effect.

The spiteful and angry words of a mother saying to her son, "I wish you had never been born" attack him in the core of his being. Likewise the anger and lack of compassion of a father, responding to the news that his unmarried daughter is pregnant, with the words "Get out of my sight, you slut," bring a crushing into her spirit.

Transference

Sometimes we handle our anger by transference or "kick the cat syndrome." We direct our anger at someone else and innocent people are made to suffer. Fearful of losing his job or not getting the pay rise or promotion he would like, a man may not confront the boss who makes unreasonable demands. He bottles up all his feelings until he comes home, but then finds fault with his wife and children and vents his anger at them.

He might even vent his anger before he gets home. If the car in front stalls at the traffic light he, still feeling angry at the boss, may blast his horn and shake his fist at the driver in a display of "road rage."

Physical aggression

Our feelings of anger can also be expressed through physical aggression. In its mildest form we may roughly handle the crockery as we do the washing up, forcefully lay the cutlery on the dining room table or bang down on the table the cup of coffee we have not so lovingly made for our spouse or colleague. Words may not be exchanged – in fact there may be a deliberate cold shouldering and a deliberate ignoring of anything spoken. An atmosphere of hostility and anger clearly exists.

Physical aggression can be directed against inanimate objects. We may slam the door or bang the table with our hands. We may throw things. The caricature of the angry wife throwing crockery against the wall in anger can be the reality for some. A man called Mark shared the following with us: "When struggling to fix my car, I would get angry and frustrated and throw my spanners into the tool box. On returning to my office from a meeting where I didn't get my way I would throw my notes across my desk in anger and frustration."

Sadly anger is often expressed in physical aggression against other people. When parents are angry, they may smack or beat the child who has somehow upset them.

The root cause of the anger that leads to a parent lashing out at a child is usually much deeper than anything the child has done or said. Sometimes the child is the innocent bystander in a row between parents. The anger one parent feels towards his or her spouse is directed at the child. Sometimes the child is the trigger to festering hurt and resentment. The husband forced into marrying his pregnant girlfriend may feel trapped and direct his anger and frustrations at the child whom he sees as the reason for his predicament.

A single teenage mum, no longer free to go clubbing with her friends, may at times see her baby as the reason why she is not enjoying life and vent her anger against the baby. Anne, a lady whom we ministered to, had been raped and abandoned by her boyfriend. The son that she subsequently bore inherited the looks of his dad. She loved her son but he eventually had to be taken into care because he was at risk from his mother's violent outbursts.

No matter what a child has done it is important for parents to learn to discipline their children when their own anger has subsided. Godly discipline comes out of love not anger.

| Godly discipline comes out of love not anger. |

In families parents sometimes vent their anger against their children, but often it is vented against their marriage partners. Anger is usually the driving force behind domestic violence. Perpetrators may justify it by saying they were provoked. The victims, often too fearful or ashamed to seek help, become passive and so the cycle is repeated. Drink is a factor in many incidences of violence.

Drinking, anger and violence are common bedfellows. The effect of alcohol is to lessen any self-control individuals may have over themselves. The anger that they have been pushing down is given free reign and manifests as a violent outburst.

These, then, are just some of the ways that we might have handled our anger in the past. In the next chapter we are going to look at some godly ways in which we can respond to and express our righteous anger in the future.

To help you think about whether anger is a problem in your life you may like to test yourself with the following checklist.

Anger checklist

Is anger a problem for you? If you are unsure, look at the list of statements on the next page and see whether any of them apply to you.

Score: Never = 0; Infrequently = 1; Sometimes = 2; Often = 3

Statement	Score
1. I find it hard to forgive someone who has hurt me.	
2. I forgive but I don't forget.	
3. When confronted I think of how to defend myself rather than listen to what is being said.	
4. In a discussion I find my voice either becoming louder or more persuasive.	
5. I become frustrated more easily than I used to.	
6. I am impatient.	
7. I am critical or judgmental of others.	
8. I avoid confrontational issues.	
9. I feel frustrated when I hear someone complain if I feel their struggles are less than mine.	
10. I feel inwardly hurt or annoyed if people around me don't recognize my needs.	
11. I continually remember negative things that have happened to me.	
12. I feel people put me down – no one listens to me.	
13. I have rows with friends and family.	
14. I have a deep desire to win – to come out on top.	
15. I slam doors, throw things, shout at people and use bad language when I'm upset.	

Analysis

- A score of more than a total of 20 would indicate that there are some unresolved anger issues in your life.
- A score greater than 30 would point to there being some major anger issues in your life.
- For each item you scored 3 ask God to show you the root reason for your feelings and/or behavior.

How Can I Express My Anger in Godly Ways?

7

The Bible acknowledges that we can have righteous anger but warns us not to sin in our anger. Many people who come for help know how to release hurt and pain through the shedding of tears but have little idea what to do with their feelings of anger. We have already discussed some of the ungodly ways we use to handle anger (chapter 6). We are frequently asked, "How can I express my anger in godly ways?" In this chapter we will consider some of these.

Talking it through

Verbalizing your thoughts and feelings with an understanding listener is often the starting point to healing. It helps you to clarify your own emotions and reactions and make some sort of sense of what you have experienced. It is particularly helpful to do this if the expression of emotions was not allowed in childhood.

> Verbalizing our feelings
> is often the starting point of healing.

Jean's testimony is a good illustration of this important principle. She writes:

"The course on anger was just what I needed to hear. I went into the course very fearful because until then anger and violence went together hand in hand. But I was amazed at the quiet and gentle way that the Lord and the teachers moved. It was a revelation to me to see that I was an angry person on the inside. For all these years I had kept it down and well hidden. But with the Lord's permission I have started to let go of it. What a release! I felt for the first time I was really being listened to. The counselors really heard me and they didn't try to rush me, in fact they said to take my time and encouraged me to talk. I thank God for them and their compassion."

A note here for those who seek to help others: as listeners we need to be empathetic to what is being said. Reflect back to the person what they have been saying. "So you felt angry when your mother...?" Such reflective feedback helps to clarify the different emotions the person may have been experiencing.

If the feelings of anger appear appropriate and righteous, the listener should speak that out in agreement with the individual sharing their story. "Yes, you had every right to feel angry about what was done to you. It was sinful and God was angry about it too." Very often there is confusion and guilt about having feelings of anger. It is reassuring for someone else to confirm that it is all right to have such feelings and that we are not sinning, or not being "good Christians," by having these feelings.

Sarah's mother would often say, "Nobody cares about me but one day I'll be dead and then you will all be sorry." Sarah used to feel angry with her mother for saying that, but then immediately felt guilty and would think that she was unkind. As we ministered to her she admitted that she felt angry with her mother but quickly added, "But that's wrong, isn't it?" Sarah was surprised to be told, "No, it's rightful anger." For the first time she realized that God didn't condemn her for her feelings of anger about her mother's manipulation and false accusations that nobody cared.

Jane was angry because a friend whom she was trying to help had cut her wrists with a piece of broken glass and had to be taken to hospital. It was as if her friend had rejected Jane and made her feel guilty about not doing enough to help. It was reassuring for Jane to be told that it was normal to feel angry in these situations and that such angry feelings were not sinful.

However, for us as listeners, when people tell us of angry feelings that are not righteous, we need to respond carefully and with wisdom. It is important that we try to understand all the facts before responding. As someone is sharing, they will be relating a mixture of righteous and unrighteous anger and behavior. As we help them to recognize righteous anger and clarify the confusion, they will often begin to recognize and be willing to repent of their unrighteous attitudes and behavior.

Our role is not to bring judgment or condemnation but to help the person be open to receive conviction from the Holy Spirit. A question such as "What do you think God feels about what happened?" gives room for a response of "He was angry" or "I don't think He would be pleased by the way I reacted."

Writing it down

Some people find it helpful to express their feelings by writing them down. We have often encouraged people to write a letter to God telling Him how they felt. This can be helpful when the person has deep-down feelings of anger towards God. It is a good idea to write down the questions that have been nagging away internally and serving as a blockage to healing. Such questions as "Where were You in all this, God?" or "Why didn't You do something to stop it?" can be verbalized for the first time and this brings a measure of healing in itself.

> David poured out his feelings to God,
> but still chose to trust Him.

In doing this we are following the example of David in the Psalms. We find him pouring out his feelings and even his resentment, anger and disappointment with God. Having done this, we find in the next breath that he is praising God and still choosing to put his trust in Him.

Shouting it out

When people have been sinned against and not allowed to express their feelings, there can be a desire inside to be heard. This can be so especially if as children they tried to tell someone what was happening to them and they were punished or not believed. There is a need not just to say that they feel angry but to shout it out to the whole world. Part of them wants to be heard. We have seen people gain a huge sense of relief and release when we have given them freedom to do this.

> The moment of anger is frozen inside.

Sometimes people don't know what words to use or how to express what they feel inside. We have probably all experienced moments of extreme frustration when our whole being has tensed up and we've said things like "I could pull my hair out" or "I could scream." For some people, that moment of extreme anger from the past has been frozen inside and may need to come out as a scream.

Susan said, "I know I needed to scream, but I'm not a person that screams. I was taught as a child that you had to keep quiet. I had this big lump inside that was so heavy and I didn't want to go home with it. Together with a member of the ministry team I threw horse chestnuts into the canal which helped me to get the screaming out. It was such a relief. I feel different now."

If you live in a flat or an apartment, it might not be too easy to "scream" out your anger without well-meaning neighbors ringing the police or wondering if they should contact the local psychiatric hospital to send you help! Where people have a need to express their anger in this way, we have sometimes encouraged them to hold a cushion or pillow close to their face and scream into it. Sometimes we have encouraged people to drive into the countryside or up into the hills where they can be alone and vent their feelings.

Creativity

Some people can express their pain and anger through a creative activity such as painting. They cannot find words, but in expressing themselves with paint, they get in touch with their inner feelings. This can be very helpful to a person experiencing a number of emotions simultaneously.

Karen painted a picture of her childhood with a thick stripe of grey paint on which she wrote the words sullen, infirmity, silly, inadequate and inferior. She then covered this grey stripe with blobs of red paint. The paint was red for anger. It was her, stamping her feet all over these years, and being angry at all the things that had happened to her.

Physical release of anger

When we feel angry our whole body tenses up. Our pulse may quicken and our blood pressure rises. Physical activity helps release the tension and anger. Many people have expressed their anger in ungodly ways by throwing things and causing damage that they later regret. There are ways we can physically release anger, without hurting ourselves or others and without the ungodly destruction of property.

> There are ways we can physically release anger without causing damage.

At Ellel Grange we have what we affectionately call the "anger tree." This is a redwood tree with a very soft bark and surrounded by mature rhododendron bushes that screen it from the rest of the garden. You can punch the trunk of this tree quite hard without damaging either your hand or the tree. Over the years this tree has witnessed many people getting in touch with and expressing their anger.

We gave Debbie a stick and she really went to town on this tree, beating the trunk with the stick and speaking out the anger she felt about all the things that her father had done to her as a child. The next day she told us that all the muscles in her arm were sore but she added, "It was worth it!"

At Ellel Grange we also have a big log pile where we keep the wood that we burn on our open fires during the winter months. Some people find release for their anger by picking up these logs and throwing them onto the top of the pile. Chopping up the logs is another way in which people find physical release for their anger.

Some people have released their anger by skimming stones across the surface of a pond or lake or throwing pebbles into the sea. One of our ministry team purchased some foam building blocks for her grandson. She discovered that throwing these released physical energy and anger with little likelihood of causing any damage.

Another safe way of dissipating tension and anger without causing damage is to take a dampened tea towel and whack the doorpost with it. There are other ways in which we can physically release anger, such as playing squash, going for a walk, kneading bread or digging the garden. In years gone by scrubbing the steps or hanging the mat on the washing line and giving it a good beating were very effective ways in which people were able to release tension and express their anger.

> We encourage the person
> to speak out their feelings of anger.

Punching pillows, pounding mattresses and beating the cushions of an armchair or a sofa can also be good ways of releasing anger. When using this method we would suggest that you kneel on the floor with your elbows resting on the chair or bed. We encourage you to speak out your feelings and express your anger. We didn't realize how much dust there can be in a chair cushion until we saw a young lady beating it as she got in touch with her buried anger about the abuse she had received!

Yet another way of releasing anger is to tear up an old telephone directory. We encourage you to rip out a page and then tear it in half again and again or screw the paper up and throw it on the floor. Don't worry about making a mess.

Priming the pump

If individuals have denied or pushed down their anger, there may be a need for what we call "priming the pump." Sometimes, as we are ministering to people, we become aware that they are struggling with great injustice and abuse that was done to them years ago. As we talk about it we can see the anger is almost on the surface. Sometimes they say it seems too big and deep or that they are frightened to let it out, in case they lose control. Often there is tremendous embarrassment. To help them, we need to demonstrate how they can express their anger in a safe way.

> Sometimes people are frightened to let their anger out, in case they lose control.

Initially we might kneel beside them in front of the sofa or start tearing out the pages from the old directory, speaking out that we are angry at the way they were treated. We say that we are angry at the things that were said to them. We say that we are angry at Satan for all the hurt and pain that he has brought into their lives.

At the same time we encourage them to speak out their own feelings. As we do this we are trying to help them express their emotions. This is not the same as some secular therapies in which people are encouraged to imagine that cushions or pillows are the people who have hurt them and to direct their anger against these substitutes. We consider this may only fuel hatred against those who have hurt them.

To move into healing, people need to get to a place where they are able to forgive those who have caused them pain. God doesn't want us to hate others, but we can hate the work of the enemy through them. We try to help the person direct their anger against the sins rather than the sinners. If they say things like "I hate you, Uncle," we gently correct them and encourage them to say instead, "I hate what you made me do..." or "I hate the words that you spoke that I was..."

Releasing of anger should not be seen as an end in itself but part of the healing process. The anger is usually a secondary emotion sitting on top of hurt, rejection, guilt and shame. The young man who threw the armchair across the foyer at Ellel Grange was expressing his anger (albeit in an ungodly way) but the pain and hurt beneath the anger came flooding to the surface. A similar thing happens as people express their anger in a godly way. As the anger is released these other emotions often surface. After someone has got in touch with and released the emotions we need to ask God to bring comfort and healing to the situations and events that are at the roots of the anger.

An important part of the healing process is to understand the role of the demonic as it relates to people with anger issues in their lives. We will look at this often misunderstood subject in the next chapter.

Lord, Why Don't You Deliver Me from My Anger?

Anger is such a powerful emotion that we can be quickly consumed by it. The words we speak and our behavior seem to be spontaneous and our will gets bypassed. After an angry outburst we often feel remorseful, sorry and ashamed that it happened. We can't recall making any choices to speak and behave as we did, it just seemed to happen.

Deliverance: part of the solution

We can look back at such incidents in our life and even say things like "I don't know what possessed me to do that" or "Something inside me seemed to take over." Such ungodly behavior, fuelled by our feelings of anger, has the hallmark of the enemy about it. The young man, for example, who wanted to strangle the speaker at the healing retreat, was being driven by more than his hurt and pain and afterwards was shocked at how he had behaved. Very often demonic power is at work in such incidents, feeding off damaged emotions, and driving us in a way that we don't fully understand.

> "I don't know what possessed me to do that."

We may cry out to God, "Lord, why don't You deliver me from my anger?" Such a prayer is a desperate plea for help. We know we have a problem but don't know how to handle it. We realize our anger is destroying our marriage and hurting the person we love. Our marriage partner loves us but has reached the end of his or her tether. The pain of separation and divorce has become a more desirable alternative than the pain of rejection and humiliation caused by our anger.

For some people a measure of deliverance will be part of the solution. Jesus came to set the captives free. He came to destroy the work of the enemy in our lives (Acts 10:38). He came to free us from slavery to sin. The freedom and release that Jesus came to bring, applies to those who are in captivity to life-controlling behavioral problems.

However, because we feel we lost control when our anger flared up, we should not be tempted to think that our problem must be purely demonic. If we say, "Something inside me took over – I just need deliverance," we may be minimizing our responsibility for what happened. Then the prayer "Lord, why don't You deliver me from my anger?" may not be so much a plea for help, but a weak excuse for what we have done. It is a blame-shifting exercise, which effectively is saying that I have this continuing problem because God has not come through for me yet.

People who have problems with anger can sometimes be looking for an instant solution. They know that a snack or a chocolate bar eaten between meals quickly gets rid of hunger. They know that taking a couple of painkillers usually gets rid of their headache quite quickly. They want a similar simple solution or instant remedy to their anger problem.

It would be wonderful if there was such a quick-fix solution to our problems with anger. It would be fantastic if we could just receive a short prayer for deliverance and see our anger problem disappear. For some the "good news" is that deliverance may be part of the solution. Their inability to win the victory in the areas of their life controlled by anger may be because they have not realized that there is a need for some deliverance.

> For some the "good news" is that deliverance
> may be part of the solution.

Following a healing retreat, Martin wrote:

"I must tell you the healing I received on the retreat was wonderful. As I drove home I just wanted to lift my hands in worship. God did so much in such a short time. The amount of restoration in my spiritual life has been phenomenal. The clinical depression has almost gone and I am weaning myself off anti-depressants. My anger has subsided enormously. My level of love and tolerance has grown substantially."

The "not so good news" is that deliverance is seldom the full solution. We need to be willing to look at the other issues involved. These may be difficult and painful to face but, unless there is that willingness to make a conscious effort and co-operate with the work of God in our lives, we will fail to move forward into victory and will remain in captivity to our anger.

Let us explain some more about the role of the demonic. We need firstly to understand how the enemy can be given rights in our lives. What do we mean by "rights"? Paul in his letter to the Christians in Ephesus warns, " 'In your anger do not sin.' . . . *do not give the enemy a foothold"* (Ephesians 4:26–27).

Giving the enemy a place

There are a number of important lessons that we can draw from these words of Paul. Firstly he is saying here that the

enemy can be given a foothold, or in other words can be given
rights in our lives. Paul is writing to Christians and warning
them that this can happen to them. The Greek word translated
"foothold" is *topos* or physical place. When the enemy has been
given a place the demonic is able to exercise something of its
nature in those areas of the person's life where it has been
given rights or authority. When this happens, we would say
that the person has a demon.

In the Bible the Greek word used for "demonized" is
daimonizomai which literally means "to have a demon" or "to
be held by a demon." Some Bible translators have wrongly
translated the word as "demon possessed." As a consequence
Christians frequently ask us the question, "Can a Christian be
demon possessed – surely I belong to Jesus?" In the sense that
possession means ownership we would agree that, as Christians, we belong to Jesus and, therefore, cannot be possessed or
owned by a demon.

We can, however, be saved or born again and still be
harboring a demon if the enemy has not been evicted. We
often liken it to buying a house. The new owner takes
possession of the house on completion of the sale but the
house may still have areas of dry rot or woodworm that need
to be treated or removed. In the same way, on conversion, the
new owner, God, takes possession of us. We are "bought with
a price" but may then need to be cleansed of anything that has
had rights in our lives.

> It can be likened to a hidden enemy
> working against a person from the inside.

What are the signs of the presence of a demon? When a
person has a demon, it can be as if there is a hidden enemy
working against them from the inside. The demonic presence
may be indicated by a strong temptation with which they are

always battling, or a sinful behavior pattern from which they struggle to break away. Sometimes it is thoughts and feelings that hinder them and stop them enjoying the abundant life.

When people react in unnecessary anger at being confronted or challenged about their sinful behavior, it is often an indication of the enemy at work in their lives. In Luke 4 we are told how Jesus went into the synagogue in His own town and challenged the people about their attitude towards Him. Their response was to become furious and seek to drive Him over the edge of a cliff (Luke 4:29). The enemy, feeding off their emotional response to Jesus' challenges, led them to want to kill Him.

Enemy footholds established through sin

The second important conclusion that we can draw from Ephesians 4:26–27 is that sin can give the demonic a foothold in our lives. Paul writes, *" 'do not sin.' . . . do not give the devil a foothold."* This scripture very clearly establishes a relationship between sinning or operating outside of God's will for our life and possible demonic consequences.

There are three ways in which sin can give the enemy a place or foothold in our lives – through our own sins, through the sins that others commit against us and through the sins of our ancestors.

Enemy rights through our own sin

When we deliberately choose to go outside God's protection and in effect choose to walk into Satan's territory, demonic footholds can be established in our lives. We can illustrate it by the picture of someone under an umbrella in a rainstorm who moves outside the protection of the umbrella and as a consequence gets wet. Here the umbrella represents God's protection. Moving away from it is what we do when we sin.

In Genesis 4 we read how God warned Cain about the consequences of his anger. Cain was jealous that Abel's sacrifice to God was more acceptable than his own. He was angry with his brother and angry with God. God told him that sin was crouching at the door. Instead of dealing with his anger he chose to express it in a violent way by murdering his brother.

> *"Sin is crouching at the door... "*
> (Genesis 4:7)

When others sin against us we can respond in sinful ways. Out of our hurt and pain we can harbor bitterness, resentment and hatred. Unless we deal with such heart attitudes, they can easily and quickly give a place to the enemy in our life. Paul recognizes this too and hence his exhortation to *"not let the sun go down while you are still angry"* (Ephesians 4:26). In other words he is encouraging us to deal in godly ways with the things that have caused us to feel angry and not to let them fester and become a feeding ground for the enemy.

Enemy rights through the sins of others

Demonic spirits can be given rights in our lives when others sin against us. These demonic rights can be likened to holes in the umbrella of protection under which we are standing. We didn't make the holes ourselves but we get wet because we are standing under them. Although we didn't sin ourselves, and were the victim of what others had done to us, the trauma, hurt and pain that we experience can provide the opportunity for the enemy to hook into.

Tom was attacked and badly beaten up by a group of young men who had been drinking. Eventually they were brought to court and given a nominal fine. Tom was scarred for years emotionally and physically by what had happened. Inside he was full of anger against the people who had attacked him and against the law system that had failed him.

> There was also a need for significant deliverance as a result of the attack.

His own responses to what happened gave the enemy some rights in his life. There was a need to repent of his own bitterness and unforgiveness towards the perpetrators of the crime against him and be released from that. There was also a need for significant deliverance as a result of the attack because he had been suffering from a great deal of fear and anxiety ever since the attack which had made him quite ill.

We have ministered to women who have, in the past, been subjected to angry attacks from their spouses or boyfriends. Frequently we have been told that their attackers have at some point gripped them by the throat and threatened to strangle them. Traumas such as these give a place to fear, rejection and sickness in the victims' lives and some deliverance is almost always necessary as part of the healing process.

Enemy rights through generational sin

A third way that demonic rights can be established in our lives is through the sins of our ancestors. While God's plan is to bring blessing through the generational line, by showing love to a thousand generations of those that love Him and keep His commandments (Exodus 20:6), the enemy, if given the opportunity, seeks to bring cursing. Exodus 20:5 states that the sins of the fathers are visited on us to the third and fourth generation and the implication from Deuteronomy 23:2 is that some sin has an effect even to the tenth generation.

It is as if the sin in one generation creates a distortion or weakness that affects future generations. The weakness would seem to give the demonic the right to try and tempt subsequent generations into the same sin. One pastor shared how he had struggled with a particular temptation all his life but had never given into it. He couldn't understand why the temptations were so strong until he had received deliverance from a demon which had come down his generational line. "I understand now," he said, "that the temptations were not just from the outside but from the inside."

> "I understand now," he said, "that the
> temptations were not just from the outside
> but from the inside."

Likewise, the anger in our life can have hereditary roots. Anger and violence can be characteristics of families, tribes and even nations. We even characterize certain people groups or families as being hot-blooded, and prone to fits of anger or violence. We may erroneously say that this is part of their personality. In fact, what we are generally observing is the outworking of Exodus 20:5 that the sins of the fathers are visited to the third and fourth generation in people's lives. God wasn't saying He will punish innocent descendants for their ancestors' sins. He was explaining that sin can pollute the children in subsequent generations.

Children imitate the behavior of adults and particularly that of their parents. If parents use their anger in ungodly ways to control or dominate others, their children will almost certainly copy this pattern of behavior. If children see their parents being angry and using physical violence against one another they will assume this is normal and acceptable behavior within marriage. Their imitated ungodly behavior gives the enemy rights in their own lives, so this is one way in which the sins of the fathers can be said to have been visited on to the children.

When a child has a temper tantrum and if, for the sake of peace and quiet, the parents give in to his demands, they are reinforcing a behavior pattern in the child. The child is learning to use anger in an ungodly way to control others. The sin or lack of discipline exercised by the parents has a consequence in the child's life.

A general outworking of Exodus 20:5 is that demons which are given a right in one generation affect the next generation. Many people who struggle with anger issues say that fits of temper, rage and violence were problems in the lives of their parents, grandparents or great grandparents. As we minister to people and they deal with the generational rights that have been given (through appropriate repentance and forgiveness), we frequently observe deliverance taking place.

Summary

In dealing with anger issues in our lives, therefore, we need to recognize that the enemy may have been given rights and that there may be some need for deliverance. However, it is seldom just a question of receiving deliverance. The underlying emotional pain needs to be dealt with. Heart attitudes, mind-sets and behavior patterns may have to be changed. We need to take away any rights that have been given to the enemy and we need to deal with those things that feed the enemy and allow him to thrive.

God wants us to be delivered from the anger issues in our lives but it involves more than just deliverance. In the next chapter we will look at the steps in the healing process.

Anger . . .
What Are the
Steps to Healing?

Handling our anger in a godly way is a challenge to all of us. Almost always there are issues from the past that are affecting the way we deal with our anger in the present. In this chapter we are going to give you some key steps in moving forward into healing and wholeness. Not every step will be applicable in every situation, so it is important for you to be asking the Holy Spirit to guide you as you read and apply them.

Step 1 – Acknowledge the problem

The first step in dealing with anger is to acknowledge that we do have a problem. Most ex-alcoholics say that they needed to get to a desperate state in which they admitted that they had a problem before they could start receiving effective treatment. It's a bit like that with anger. We need to recognize and acknowledge that we have a problem and then own it.

In our hearts we need to have a desire to be right with God, whatever it takes. We need to want to be transformed into the image of Jesus. We need to be open to the convicting power of the Holy Spirit. We need to take down defense barriers of self-justification and allow God to speak into our hearts and show us when our thoughts or behaviors are out of line with His.

> In our hearts we need to have a desire to be
> right with God, whatever it takes.

We may need to be prepared to make ourselves vulnerable and give others permission to bring godly correction. When we do this we need to be willing to listen to correction such as "I think you need to take time out to cool down" without allowing it to feed our anger even more!

Step 2 – Analyze the problem

The second step in dealing with our problems of anger is to try and determine why we are feeling angry. In the heat of the moment this is not easy. We have to ask God to help us to slow down our responses. When we find we are feeling angry we need to get into the habit of saying nothing and taking time out to evaluate why we are feeling and reacting the way we are.

Here are some helpful questions to consider as you analyze your reactions and behavior:

1. What are the circumstances or triggers that lead to me feeling angry?
2. Why do I feel angry?
   - Do I feel rejected?
   - Do I feel betrayed?
   - Do I feel undervalued?
   - Do I feel something is unjust?
   - Do I feel controlled and dominated?
   - Do I feel that my goals are being blocked?
3. Are my feelings of anger righteous? Is God angry about the things I feel angry about?

4. Have I responded in an ungodly way?
5. Have I perceived the circumstances correctly?
6. Are there some past issues feeding into this problem?
   Ask yourself, "Has this sort of thing happened before?"

Think about the last time you felt angry or reacted out of anger. Go through the above questions asking God to bring you revelation about what happened, how you felt and how you behaved.

Step 3 – Forgive those who have caused you to feel angry

Perhaps the most important step in dealing with the root causes of our anger is to forgive all those who have hurt us and thus caused us to feel angry. This is not easy to do, but it is what Jesus asks us to do. Unless we forgive we will remain chained to the past and unable to move forward.

> Unless we forgive we will remain chained to the past and unable to move forward.

Following her healing retreat Brenda wrote the following:

"I had a bad relationship with both my parents, and was abused as a child by my father. I always suffered rejection and as a result became a very closed person, unable to trust anyone. Aggression and anger had been suppressed within. I also suffered from bouts of depression and sometimes contemplated suicide. In an act of my will I forgave those I needed to, including my parents. This began the emotional forgiveness process. All I can say is 'Praise God!' I'm more peaceful, I don't get aggressive and worked up any more, and I'm not depressed."

Forgiveness is not minimizing or condoning what was done to us. Forgiveness is not denying the feelings we have about what happened. It is OK to feel angry about what happened and to express that anger in a godly way. Forgiveness is not erasing or forgetting the past. It is not forgiving and forgetting. Rather forgiveness is more like lancing a painful boil. It allows the poison to be released. There may still be a scar but not the severe pain.

Forgiveness does not mean that we have to trust the person who has hurt us. The person will have to earn that trust. Forgiveness is not pardoning a person and saying that their sin against us is no longer punishable. Only God can pardon someone in that sense. When God does this He is not saying that the sin is not punishable but rather that Jesus has Himself taken the punishment for the sin.

Forgiveness of others means granting a person more mercy than they deserve, just as Jesus has shown us more mercy than we deserve. Forgiveness means dismissing bitterness and resentment from our hearts. Forgiveness means giving up our desire for revenge and retaliation. When we are hurt, our carnal nature wants us to get our own back – to inflict punishment on the person who has hurt us. We want to judge the person and execute the sentence upon them.

> Forgiveness means giving up our desire
> for revenge and retaliation.

Forgiveness, however, means releasing the person from our judgment as to what the penalty should be. It is like handing the case to a higher authority to deal with. When we release someone into the freedom of our forgiveness we are handing them over to God. We do this in the knowledge that God will deal with the person in a just and righteous way.

We need to recognize that forgiveness starts in the will. It is a choice that we make. We might not feel like forgiving but we choose to line up our will with God's will for our lives. Forgiveness comes out of a heart attitude that wants to be right with God. Making this choice to forgive allows the healing process to start.

When we forgive we need to try to separate between the sin and the sinner. Doing this helps us to direct our anger against what was done to us rather than against the person who did it. We are not trying to excuse the person for what they did but this separation will help us to deal with our heart response to what happened.

We need to ask Jesus to help us to forgive. In our human nature we don't want to forgive. We need to ask Jesus for His heart of forgiveness. We need some of the forgiveness that Jesus had that enabled Him to pray, "Father, forgive them for they know not what they do." Ask Jesus to help you see the person as Jesus sees them – a sinner worth dying for. We can speak out our forgiveness in a prayer such as this:

> *Thank You, Jesus, for dying that I might be forgiven. By an act of my will I now choose to forgive those who have hurt me or caused me to feel angry* (at this point you should name them out loud). *I release each and every one of these people into the freedom of my forgiveness. In Jesus' name. Amen.*

Forgiveness is a process and we have to keep choosing to walk in that forgiveness. Each time we remember the pain or injustice that we experienced, we need to continue to choose to forgive the people involved.

Step 4 – Repent of any ungodly response that you have made out of your anger

No matter what others have done to us we need to respond in godly ways. This does not mean that we shouldn't feel angry, but it does mean that our response should be godly. If we have responded in an ungodly way we need to confess and repent. To confess means to agree with God's verdict on what we have done. It is taking responsibility for what we have done without blaming others.

> Repentance does not mean that
> we shouldn't feel angry.

To repent means to turn away from the things that we did that were wrong. It is telling God that if the same circumstances arose we would not want to respond in the same way. If a woman still smiles and gets satisfaction out of having damaged her husband's car, when she discovered he was having an affair behind her back, or says, "I would do the same again if I discovered my spouse cheating on me," she hasn't reached that place of true repentance.

It is reality that in the same circumstances she might still feel like damaging his car or worse. However, true repentance is getting to a place where she can say that she will ignore such feelings and desires for retaliation but instead will exercise her freedom of choice to do what is godly rather than that which is ungodly.

The following prayer can be used as a basis for bringing these issues before God:

> *Father, I confess that as a result of being hurt I have allowed myself to sin by* _____ (be specific and name ungodly attitudes, thinking patterns and behavior). *I acknowledge my sin and I now repent and turn from it, asking that You will forgive me and cleanse me. In Jesus' name. Amen.*

If we have blamed God for what has happened in our lives and been angry with God, we need to recognize our wrongdoing in this. God loves us and wants the best for us. We may not understand all that happens to us but we need to get angry with the enemy of our soul, who delights in the bad things that happen to us, rather than blame God.

Take a moment to consider whether you have been angry with God and blamed Him for things that Satan or other people have done. This type of prayer may help:

> *Please forgive me, Lord, for blaming You for what others have done to me. I know that You hate what Satan has done in my life. Thank You for loving me and promising to set me free. Amen.*

Maybe as a consequence of being hurt by others, you have internalized your anger against yourself. You may have done this by self-harming or by contemplating or attempting suicide. Such thoughts and actions are ultimately a rejection of who you are. It is a rejection of yourself as a valued and precious creation of God.

Such rejection of yourself is doing the work of Satan for him. His objectives are to steal and destroy. If we have done these things we need to bring them before the Lord in confession and repentance. You can do this with a prayer such as:

> *Thank You, Father, for my life and for creating me as me. Thank You, Jesus, that You love me so much that You died in order that I might have life. I now repent of wanting to die and renounce the contract I made with Satan by wishing I were dead. I now choose life and take away from Satan every right to my life that I gave him by my attitudes or desires. I now choose to live for Jesus and make Him Lord of every area of my life. In Jesus' name. Amen.*

Step 5 – Breaking of ungodly ties

When relationships go wrong and are outside of God's plans to bring blessing to one another, ungodly bonds or ties are created. Such ungodly ties are formed in any relationship where the individuals agree to operate in rebellion to God's law or where one or both of the individuals sin against the other.

> Ungodly ties can be likened to chains
> binding us to other individuals.

These ties can be likened to ungodly chains binding us to that other individual. It is as if part of our being is intermingled with theirs and part of their being is intermingled with ours. Their hurtful words and wrong actions against us can be like an unending tape recording playing in our mind and holding us in captivity to the events of the past.

After having repented of expressing our anger in a wrong way towards others and also having forgiven specifically any who have hurt us in any way, there is a need to break any ungodly ties that have been formed. A prayer such as the following can be used:

> *I ask You, God, to break the ungodly tie existing between me and* _____ (name the individuals). *I ask that You sever that linking and completely separate out and restore to me every part of myself which has been wrongfully tied to* _____ (name the individuals). *I ask this in Jesus' name. Amen.*

Step 6 – Inner healing and godly expression of the anger

In chapter 8 we looked at godly ways in which we can express our anger. It is often appropriate to do this as part of the healing process. It is good sometimes to speak out a prayer

giving God permission to bring release and healing to our
emotions.

We find that during ministry people need to be encouraged
not to be fearful but trust that Jesus will help them face and
deal with their emotions in a way that they are able to cope
with. The following prayer is a good one, if you recognize that
you may have denied or buried your emotions and submits
your healing to Jesus:

Father God, I thank You for my emotions.

*I confess that I have not always recognized or fully
accepted my emotions or properly understood their place in
how You made me.*

*I confess that I have not expressed my emotions correctly –
I have pushed them down, ignored them, or allowed them
uncontrolled reign. As a result I have caused hurt to others.
Please forgive me for doing this.*

*I confess that I have sometimes used my emotions and my
anger in ungodly ways and sought to control and manipulate others through my emotional behavior. I repent of doing
this and ask You to forgive me.*

*I ask You now, Father, to help me express my emotions
and buried feelings in godly ways. I choose to face the
hurt and pain and give You permission to bring Your healing
into these areas of my life.*

I ask these things in the name of my Lord Jesus. Amen.

After having prayed this prayer, allow God to put you in touch
with releasing your hurt, pain and anger.

For some people this step will be the most important part
of moving forward. For some there will be a need to express
some of the well of emotional pain before they can forgive.
In the midst of facing and expressing the pain we need to
continue to speak out forgiveness of those who have hurt
us.

Step 7 – Dealing with ancestral sin

If you believe that anger and violence in your life has a hereditary root you need to deal with this by forgiving your ancestors for anything they have done which has affected you and by renunciation of their sinful practices. You can do this using a prayer such as the following:

> *Thank You, Jesus, that You have rescued me from the dominion of darkness and brought me into Your wonderful light. You have redeemed me with Your precious blood and I belong to You. I have been born again and I am a member of the family of God. Jesus is my Lord!*
>
> *I am also a member of a human family and I thank You for them. I acknowledge and confess that I and my forbears have sinned and broken Your laws. We have done this in thought, word and deed and, in particular, by involvement in _____.*
>
> *I forgive my forbears for the consequences of their sins that have been visited into my life. I take responsibility for the ways in which I have repeated their sins and I repent before You and ask Your forgiveness.*
>
> *Thank You, Jesus, that by Your death You have redeemed me and loosed me from the curse of generational iniquity and that, in You, I have chosen to identify myself wholeheartedly with God's family and thereby inherit every promise and blessing that comes from Him. In Jesus' name. Amen.*

> "Thank You, Jesus, that You have redeemed me and loosed me from the curse of generational iniquity."

Forgiveness like that is the first step to freedom from any demonic influence that could have come to you through your family line. We find in ministry it is helpful to ask God to break any ungodly tie between you and your parents and the ancestral lines through which demonic rights may have been given. This can be done using a prayer along these lines:

> *In the name of Jesus I ask You, God, to break all the ungodly ties that have been established between me and my father (mother) and my paternal (maternal) line. I ask that You sever that linking and completely separate out and restore to me every part of myself which has been wrongfully tied to anyone in the paternal (maternal) line.*

Step 8 – Deliverance

Where the enemy has been given rights in our lives as a result of our sins against others, or the sins of others affecting us (including those of our ancestors), there may be a need for deliverance. Before attempting deliverance it is important that the enemy's rights to be there are taken away through confession, repentance and renunciation of sin, and forgiveness of those who have sinned against us.

Because the demonic latches into and feeds off emotional pain, it is preferable in most instances first to bind up the demonic and deal with the healing of inner pain and to express the emotion of anger in a godly way before casting out the demonic. When attempting deliverance, especially where inner healing issues have not first been dealt with, strong manifestations and violent outbursts that are difficult to control may be encountered. After dealing with the inner healing issues the individual receiving ministry will often just give a deep sigh or something similar as the demonic is addressed and expelled.

Although freedom from demonic bondage can be achieved through self-deliverance, we would generally recommend that you ask someone with understanding and experience in this area to pray with you.

During ministry the person receiving deliverance needs to be encouraged to exercise their will and authority in telling the enemy to leave. The demonic can be addressed in the following way:

> **In the name of Jesus I command the unclean spirit of**
> **_____** (name the area of bondage)
> **to leave _____** (name the person)
> **without hurting or harming them or any other person**
> **and without going into any other member of their family.**
> **In Jesus' name. Amen.**

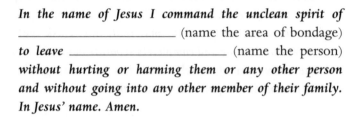

The important thing is to know and exercise
the authority that we have in Jesus
to deal with the enemy.

The actual words used are relatively unimportant. The important thing is to know and exercise the authority that we have in Jesus to deal with the enemy once his rights to be there have been removed.

Step 9 – Reconciliation

When relationships have been damaged as a result of ungodly expression of our anger there will be a need for reconciliation. Taking responsibility for our action, and asking the person we have wronged to forgive us, can be an important step forward.

Even if what the other person did was wrong, there is still a need to say that we are sorry for the way we responded, if we responded in an unhelpful way. When we humble ourselves in this way we are not condoning what they did to make us feel angry. We are not saying that we are going to start trusting them again immediately – they may have to earn that trust. We are not saying that we will submit to their ungodly control and domination. What we are doing is trying to get our heart right before God. As we do this God often starts to move in the heart of the other person to bring healing of the relationship.

A key to reconciliation is understanding how to confront others in a godly way, which is the subject of the next chapter.

How Can I Confront in Love?

As we seek to live godly lives, it is in our relationships with others that we are most likely to experience feelings of anger and ungodly reactions.

Yes, we can get frustrated with the car or computer that breaks down, the public services that are inefficient or the failure of governing authorities to tackle issues that we value highly. However, it is in our day-to-day dealings with our families, friends, casual acquaintances and those that we work with that anger more often arises. It is almost always within the context of relationships that we are hurt by others and express our feelings in ungodly ways.

Confront the issue and/or the person

Wives might be irritated by the irksome way their husbands drop dirty clothes around the house or students by the fact that their flatmates never seem to do their share of the chores. We might be annoyed by the way our boss takes us for granted in the things he asks us to do or the way that our colleagues at work borrow our stapler and never remember to return it. Unless we confront the issues, however, and the people creating them, our lives will be dominated by expressed or suppressed anger.

> Unless we confront the issues, and the people
> creating them, our lives will be dominated by
> expressed or suppressed anger.

Confrontation is a very emotive word. Most people's idea of confronting is formed from past memories of aggressive, hostile arguments which they witnessed and it is something they are very eager to avoid at all costs in the future. One of the parties has normally been the more powerful, causing the other one to yield and give up, often with an embarrassing loss of control, such as a display of angry emotions or leaving the room overwhelmed by tears.

In future "losers" may choose never to express their true feelings and may agree to whatever is wanted without discussion. One of the ways to find out whether you are being dominated, manipulated or controlled by someone is to ask whether you are afraid to speak out when you disagree. You may think, "I might get hurt and rejected"; "It will do no good, the relationship will be destroyed"; "It will cost me too much effort"; "I might look foolish"; or even "I might hurt and crush the other person." It is amazing how the "what ifs" build up within the mind and cause a blockage.

We can think of many reasons why we shouldn't confront, but avoiding confrontation may not be the godly way of handling the situations that we face. Before looking at how we can confront in love, let us first look at the other options which are open to us when someone hurts us or makes us feel angry.

Peace at all costs

When our anger has been aroused in our relationships with others, the first option we have is to keep our feelings to ourselves. If we feel angry about something we are asked to do, we can choose not to express our feelings but to submit passively. If we are hurt and angered by things said to us we can feign indifference and keep silent. We may adopt a "peace at any cost" approach and avoid risking any confrontation.

> There may be peace on the outside
> but it is at the cost of disquiet and
> turmoil on the inside.

We may go away and think over and over about what happened, trying to shrug it off and minimize the hurt and pain. We might even have a drink or treat ourselves to a chocolate cake to cheer ourselves up. We may blame ourselves or convince ourselves that avoiding confrontation was the best solution. This way of dealing with our feelings of anger becomes an established behavior pattern. There may be peace on the outside but it is invariably at the cost of disquiet and turmoil on the inside.

Tell the world

A second option we have when we have been hurt and angered by someone is to make sure everyone else knows how badly we have been treated. We tell anyone who will listen, how righteous we are, and how unrighteous the people are who have offended us. We attempt to paint a glowing picture of our own behavior and character whilst trying to assassinate that of others.

> People who react in this way are usually hostile
> and aggressive themselves.

This is most certainly not the right way to handle relationship difficulties. It can easily become gossip or slander and destroys rather than builds relationships. People who react in this way are usually hostile and aggressive themselves. They would probably say that they enjoy confrontation and putting the world to rights. It may be that their own attitudes created or fuelled the situation that led to them feeling angry and badly treated in the first place.

Overlooking the issue

The third option we have in resolving situations that make us angry is not to confront the other person but to choose to overlook any offence we may feel. The Bible says, *"love covers over a multitude of sins"* (1 Peter 4:8). In processing our thoughts, we may decide to overlook the grievance we have against another, decide that we can go on with the relationship and that nothing needs to be changed. We choose to adjust our values and assessment of the situation in some way to find a place of peace.

We might decide that we are going to allow our friend to have a few minor quirks and be tolerant of faults which inconvenience us in a small way. We decide that he or she has many wonderful qualities which more than compensate for such trivial causes of irritation. The golden rule of love explains that we are to treat others as we would like them to treat us (Matthew 7:12). We can choose to apply 1 Corinthians 13 and not keep a record of wrongs. We can choose not to accumulate the anger and resentment caused by minor irritations.

> If we are not choosing to overlook some faults in others, we may need to examine our own hearts.

Our decision to overlook the issue is not taken because we fear confronting other people with their shortcomings, but because we have a measure of mercy and grace which we want to bestow upon them as a gift. We choose to exercise forbearance and be tolerant. We choose to have patience, which is one of the nine fruits of the Holy Spirit, and is one of the aspects of true love.

Overlooking some of the faults we see in others is part of life. We are all unique and differ in our values. If we don't choose to overlook some faults, and feel everything we find irritating needs confronting, we may need to examine our own hearts. Have we become critical and over-judgmental? Are we trying to control the environment around us? Are we putting our needs above the needs of others? Do we allow others to confront us or are we the ones doing all the confrontation?

Choosing to confront in love

The fourth option when someone hurts us or causes us to feel angry is to choose to confront in love. This option sounds like a contradiction in terms. Can confrontation be an act of love? Can it help the relationship and will it be the best way forward for both the injured party and the perpetrator?

> Confrontation can be loving, sensitive and gentle.

Confrontation need not be an aggressive or hostile action, as many imagine, but can be loving, sensitive and gentle. Ephesians 4:15 says that we are to speak the truth in love. Jesus gave us many good examples of confrontation when He spoke to people about their sin.

For example, Jesus challenged the woman at the well with the truth about herself, but gently and lovingly with a perfect understanding of her hurt and pain. This is an example of confrontation, but the conversation was done in private, with due consideration of how embarrassed she might be if others were present.

Jesus loved His disciples but there were times when He rebuked them for their wrong heart attitudes, for instance when James and John wanted to call down fire upon a Samaritan village in punishment for rejecting Jesus (Luke 9:54–55).

With the Pharisees, Jesus often expressed His disapproval in very strong terms. The time for gentleness was over because these religious leaders could no longer be reached by soft words. Their hearts were hard, insensitive and full of evil, so Jesus spoke as a righteous judge.

From time to time you may have heard a preacher say, "When someone does something wrong and sins against you, all you have to do is follow the biblical guidelines in Matthew 18:15–17."

> *"If your brother sins against you, go and show him his fault, just between the two of you. If he listens to you, you have won your brother over. But if he will not listen, take one or two others along, so that 'every matter may be established by the testimony of two or three witnesses.' If he refuses to listen to them, tell it to the church; and if he refuses to listen even to the church, treat him as you would a pagan or a tax collector."*
>
> (Matthew 18:15–17)

The reality of applying this principle, however, is far from simple where human relationships have become marred by sinful behavior patterns. Perhaps the brother doing the sinning is a very dominating and aggressive individual. Perhaps you, as the injured party, are fearful of receiving further wounding or rejection if you confront someone who has hurt you.

If, for example, you were deeply rejected in childhood you may feel quite insecure and struggle with feelings of low self-esteem. When someone falsely tells you that you have done something wrong, you may be confused and unable to understand whether the accusation against you is true or false. You may feel angry about the false accusation, but lack the confidence to confront the accuser. The accusation may tap into the false burden of guilt and shame which you are already carrying. You may even begin to feel it was your fault.

> Take someone else along for protection and support
> when there might be a danger of intimidation.

Despite such difficulties we all need to seriously consider the words of Jesus about bringing matters into the open. The Bible gives guidelines of what to do if your brother does not listen to you. This could be interpreted as taking someone else along for protection and support when there might be a danger of intimidation, and someone is likely to behave in an unreasonable manner.

In following biblical guidelines to work towards resolving relationship problems and to aim at reconciliation, we would do well to heed what Jesus taught in Matthew 7. He said that it is only after we have taken the plank out of our own eye, that we are able to see clearly and help remove the speck of dust from our brother's eye. We are to be humble and willing to recognize our own faults and shortcomings before we try to bring some challenge or confrontation to others about their behavior. Forgiveness deals with the past and is something which all of us are commanded to do. However, for there to be reconciliation in a relationship today there needs to be some action and communication by both of the people involved.

The language of confrontation

When confronting others the language we use is very important. We need to express why we feel hurt and angry. We need to explain our understanding of the situation, recognizing that we may not have got all the facts right. We need to avoid an accusatory style which may only provoke a defensive response. Rather than say, "You made me angry yesterday when you...," it is better to say something like, "I felt angry and put down yesterday when you said..." Focus on your own feeling rather than blaming.

Sensitive and empathetic people will respond to softly spoken words of confrontation. Generally they will recognize that you feel hurt by something that has happened and will want to work towards reconciliation and an amicable solution. Insensitive people, on the other hand, may not even notice they are being challenged and rebuked. The style might have to be much stronger in these cases.

> Stay calm and don't get drawn into
> a verbal slanging match.

Suppose the person laughs at you or ignores you? We would urge you not to give up trying to communicate but to send another message about how you feel such as, "I feel that you do not understand how hurt I'm feeling." We recommend that you keep communicating truthfully until the person hears you. What if the person gets angry? Stay calm yourself and do not get drawn into a verbal slanging match. Don't back down but say something like, "Perhaps you need time to think about what I have said. Maybe we can talk about it some more tomorrow."

A controlling or aggressive person may try to defend themselves by attacking you further. Quietly but firmly hold to your position without wavering. It will require determination to resolve the issue. If the person walks out, pick up the subject again later on without comment about their reaction. Stick to one issue and avoid inappropriate humor. Say, "From my perspective it seems..." Don't make assumptions but listen carefully, without interruption, to the other person to check whether you have got things right.

Before confronting

It is seldom easy to confront someone and it can be quite daunting. Take time to prepare.

1. Get in touch with your own feelings.
2. Think it over and don't rush into anything.
3. Pray for wisdom.
4. Identify the true cause of your anger. Clarify the issues. Perhaps talk it over with a trusted friend or counselor.
5. Evaluate whether your anger is rightful.
6. Try to understand why the other person behaved in the way they did.
7. Decide what to do.
8. If you decide the best way forward is to confront the person, do it gently without attacking and do it in private. If they are too intimidating or there is a danger of being abused, it may be necessary to take someone else with you.

Plan how you might broach the subject. You might want to say, "I'd like to have a talk with you. When would be a good time?" or "It's about yesterday. I don't know if you realize that I felt quite hurt when you said I was too controlling and that no one would want to work with me in future" or "I felt hurt last week when you said I was undermining your authority" or "There seems to be a misunderstanding between us."

> Take comfort and assurance
> from knowing that we are trying to do
> what Jesus would have us do.

When we confront, remember that we are not out to win points or an argument. We are not necessarily looking for an apology. We are doing it to clear the air and for the good of our ongoing relationship with the person. Whatever the outcome we can take comfort and assurance from knowing that we are trying to do what Jesus would have us do.

Anger . . . How Will You Handle It?

In this book we have attempted to present a biblical understanding of anger. We have looked at the causes of anger and the steps to dealing with anger issues in your life. Hopefully these steps will have given you insight and helped you to identify and deal with the root causes of your anger. Hopefully they will also have helped you deal with the unresolved and unexpressed anger in your life that has fuelled your feelings and behavior in the past.

It is inevitable, however, that you will in future face situations in which you will feel angry. The challenge facing you is to start to deal with these issues without falling back into your previous behavior patterns. If you have dealt with the backlog of anger in your life you will be able to do this more successfully but you will still have to keep on exercising your will and making right decisions.

Allow God to have complete control

Choose to make Jesus Lord of every area of your life. Earnestly desire that your thoughts, emotions and behavior in every situation will be the thoughts, emotions and behavior that Jesus would experience if facing the same situation.

> *Clothe yourself with the Lord Jesus Christ,*
> *and do not think about how to gratify*
> *the desires of the sinful nature.*
> (Romans 13:14)

Ask Jesus to help you to use your anger as a motivating force for change. If the anger is connected with some unhealed hurts in your life don't ignore the hurts but seek to have them healed. If the anger is relating to injustices from others, then ask God to show you how He wants you to respond to the injustices. If the anger stems from relationships and the way others have treated you, let your anger motivate you to work at bringing about change and improving that relationship. Think about what is wrong with the situation and then about how it could be changed. Keep this picture in your mind as you work towards solving the problems.

Take full responsibility for your behavior

Choose that in future you will recognize that there is a difference between anger as a feeling and anger as behavior. Resolve that you will take responsibility for your ungodly behavior arising out of anger.

Choose that in future you will not blame-shift, or try to justify your ungodly behavior. Instead, seek to exercise self-control. Ask God to slow down your impulsive aggressive attitudes and behavior when you feel threatened or angered. Resolve that if you do fail you will be humble enough to seek forgiveness and to seek reconciliation.

Choose to deal with anger as it comes up

Choose to deal with anger issues as they come up, rather than deny or suppress them. Unless you do this you will again build

> *"In your anger do not sin":*
> *Do not let the sun go down while you are still angry.*
> (Ephesians 4:26)

up a backlog of anger that will feed ungodly thoughts and behavior.

Choosing to deal with anger does not mean that you have to deal with issues the instant you feel angry. You may have to take time out to calm down. It does mean that you choose to analyze the reason for the anger and, if appropriate, express that anger. It means being honest with yourself and dealing with all unrighteous aspects of your anger and choosing to be motivated by righteous anger.

Walk in release and forgiveness

Choose to walk in forgiveness of those who hurt you or upset you. This does not mean that you don't feel angry at the sins they commit against you, but that you choose to exercise mercy and grace towards them.

> *Bear with each other and forgive whatever grievances you may have against one another. Forgive as the Lord forgave you.*
> (Colossians 3:13)

It means that you choose to treat others as God treats you. Choose that you will dismiss resentment and bitterness from your heart towards those that hurt you. Choose to see others as God sees them – sinners in need of forgiveness.

Practice godly confrontation

Determine that you will not remain a victim when others attempt to control, manipulate or abuse you. Choose that you will recognize the anger you feel in such situations and decide that you will no longer be passive but active.

Choose that with God's help you will overcome your fear and practice godly confrontation. Choose that you will try to clarify misunderstandings which lead to confusion and mixed emotional reactions. Choose that you will try to express to others the reason why their words or actions have given rise to feelings of anger within you.

Seek to live in the presence of God

Seek to know God's presence with you day by day. Choose that you will be a person who will worship and praise God irrespective of circumstances. Choose to be controlled by the Spirit of God rather than the carnal nature. Choose to be quick to call out for God's help when those feelings of anger come to the surface.

> *Dear Lord Jesus, You know everything about me. You know all the struggles that I have with my emotions and my expression of them. Lord, help me to become more like You. Help me to recognize and understand my feelings and to react to them in the way that You would react. Help me, Lord, to apply into my life all the things that You have shown me. Help me, Lord, to co-operate with the work of the Holy Spirit in my life that I might be transformed into Your image. Amen.*

As you put into practice the keys and the principles shared in this book our prayer and hope for you is that your answer to the question "Anger ... How Will You Handle It?" will be, "Much better than I did in the past."

We hope you enjoyed reading this Sovereign World book.
For more details of other Sovereign books and
new releases see our website:

www.sovereignworld.com

If you would like to help us send a copy of this book
and many other titles to needy pastors in the Third World,
please write for further information or send your gift to:

Sovereign World Trust
PO Box 777
Tonbridge, Kent TN11 0ZS
United Kingdom

You can also visit **www.sovereignworldtrust.com**.
The Trust is a registered charity.

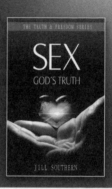